LEXICON OF
WATER GARDENS

Attractive designs and appropriate plantings

Hermann Hackstein &
Wota Wehmeyer

© 2005 Rebo International b.v., Lisse, The Netherlands
1st edition 2006 Rebo Publishers

Author: Herman Hackentein & Wota Wehmeyer
Typesetting: AdAm Studio, Prague, The Czech Republic
Translator: Karen Green for First Edition Translations Ltd,
Cambridge, UK
Editor: Kay Hyman for First Edition Translations Ltd
Proofreading: Sarah Dunham

ISBN 90 366 1891 6

Contents

Introduction

FOR THE LOVE OF IT

It's said that keen water gardeners know every single drop of water in their ponds intimately. Of course this is an exaggeration, but there is a grain of truth at the heart of it, because those who are passionately devoted to their water features do know them inside out.

It's not just oddballs who take their water gardening to extremes. A great many gardeners who have installed a pond or water course dedicate themselves to it wholeheartedly because the fascination with incorporating water into a garden design, and the possibilities it offers are enormous, varied, and attractive. This book hopes to convey just a small part of what makes gardening with water so appealing. It's not just for giving factual information, or providing hints and suggestions. As well, this book aims to highlight and explain the fascination with water in gardens.

The photographs in the first section of the book are the most important element we use to achieve this. They don't just provide a visual explanation of the text on siting and designing water features; at the same time they convey the atmosphere that permeates a garden with water, the feelings of peace and relaxation that are evoked, as well as the beauty and inner strength that are invariably associated with these gardens. The same applies to the plant descriptions in the book's second section.

There is not enough space in this volume to introduce every plant that grows in or near water, and it is therefore not as comprehensive as an encyclopedia. Instead there are suggestions on how to bring a water feature to life.

The choice of plants does reflect the authors' preferences. Of course, an "expert" will note the absence of this or that plant that he or she considers especially important, but perhaps there will be plants never before considered, and which are equally capable of bringing long-term enrichment.

As in Section One, the plant descriptions do not simply convey factual gardening knowledge, such as flowering period and height. They should be regarded as snapshots taken with the aim of putting a little of the allure of water gardening within everyone's grasp and conveying additional background information in an accessible way—in other words, an enjoyable read!

The fascination with water

A VALUABLE ADDITION TO YOUR GARDEN

Incorporating water into a garden design is one of the most exciting opportunities for enriching a garden with a natural attraction, because the primal power of this element and its natural aura are coupled with an almost inexhaustible fund of new gardening possibilities.

The available design options are hugely varied, starting with a little container, planted up as a mini-pond, or just a deep, wide dish in which floats a single, beautiful plant. Stones with water bubbling out of them or individual water features that are anchored in the garden are easy not just on the eyes, but on the ear too, and are somewhat livelier to look at.

The first step towards a full-scale water feature is a little pond which, in just a few square feet, can provide a home in and out of the water for a whole range of different plants. At the opposite end of the spectrum is a garden with a stream, where the cool wetness runs into separate pools before culminating in a large pond with a wide variety of fauna and flora.

The sheer, never-ending versatility of designing gardens which incorporate that primal element, water, is not enough to explain their great popularity. There are

many other aspects that must be taken into consideration, starting with the element's characteristics. When the wind ruffles the surface of a pond, when the skies are reflected therein, or when, or the water flows gently through a lovingly designed water course, the eye catches on something almost magical.

Add to this a pleasingly designed pond or stream, incorporated with finesse into the garden's landscape and lovingly planted, and the result is a natural work of art that presents the viewer with a wealth of eye-catching facets.

RESTORATIVE VALUE

Water in the garden is calming and relaxing. Seated comfortably beside a garden pond, your thoughts soon wander, everyday cares fade away, and you experience that beneficial feeling of peace and relaxation. A well-designed water feature can prove to be an oasis where body and mind can recuperate quickly. It can also be a source of strength that inspires the feelings of well-being and repose that are rarely experienced anywhere else but on holiday.

FAVORABLE SOIL CONDITIONS

It is not only man that benefits from a garden pond or water course, but also all the plants in the immediate vicinity. The increased humidity that water contributes promotes plants' growth, health and strength. Shades of green along the banks will be especially rich, and blooms will last longer. Even frosts will be less hard, because to a certain extent the water inhibits the cold.

An appropriately designed water garden can open up an extremely diverse habitat for numerous animals and microorganisms—primarily many freshwater fish. Choosing them and settling them in, observing them, caring for them, and breeding them is surely a reward in itself. But the world of water is not associated only with the shimmering scales of goldfish, koi carp, and others; garden ponds or water courses provide room

for many creatures to grow and multiply, from little amphibians to big frogs, from pond skaters to dragonflies—an irresistible invitation to take a closer look at Nature.

HORTICULTURAL POSSIBILITIES

From the queen of aquatic plants, the water lily, to rasses and reeds, to inconspicuous underwater plants—hundreds of species flourish in and near water. Pond and water course thus offer a unique opportunity of incorporating varied, often breathtakingly beautiful plants into the garden, and expanding the horticultural perspective with interesting alternatives.

In addition, the inclusion of water has a decisive influence on overall garden design. It doesn't matter whether it's a pond or water course, ornamental pool, or fountain—the site must be

planted and placed carefully in relation to the garden's other features.

Water can create separate zones that harmonize with other garden elements while simultaneously contrasting with them. Water is not just a separate design tool; it also links and integrates, enriching the overall garden space with a useful attraction.

MORE REASONS

There are many other reasons, in addition to these primary aspects, why so many people want to use water in their gardens, including, for example, designing the garden according to the principles of the Asian philosophy *feng shui*, which creates a world of adventure for children, or planting a biotope that creates a refuge for native animals and plants.

Whatever the motivation for incorporating water into the design of your "outdoor room," ultimately it's a matter of personality and individual preference. This explains why every water feature is different.

SPECIFIC WATER FEATURE DESIGN

Specific garden designs come in many types, and there is a certain kind of water feature to suit each, whether it is a pond, running water, or a small container.

COTTAGE GARDENS

Cottage gardens are brought alive by the colorful variety of different flowering shrubs which, together with roses and summer bedding plants, create a romantic ensemble. They are usually enriched by numerous useful plants such as herbs, soft fruit bushes, and espaliered orchard fruit.

Recommended water designs include small, naturalistic ponds or water courses. The area of water should not dominate, but the pond and/or water course, as a separate design feature, should merge harmoniously into the overall setting. In the process particular attention should be paid to the bog areas and marginal planting.

Suitable styles that fit perfectly into the atmosphere of a cottage garden include a walled round well, or a water trough. Springs, or stones with water bubbling out of them, predominantly in natural materials, are recommended features that incorporate running water.

FORMAL GARDENS

The formal garden is not so much characterized by individual plants, as by clear lines and directions. There are sharp distinctions between the pathways and dividing areas. The parks and gardens surrounding the great houses of the aristocracy are classic examples of this type of garden, although modern garden architecture also looks to clear and unambiguous lines.

The first choice in this case should be ornamental ponds in formal basins, which echo the lines of the garden as a whole. They can be combined to superb effect with reflecting pools of water and/or fountains.

JAPANESE GARDENS

Gardens as meditative spaces are modeled on those from the Far East. Carefully arranged areas of gravel and stone, pagodas, and pavilions form a harmonious unit. Purposefully placed water courses and

pools are essential to a Japanese garden—especially if it is designed on the principles of feng shui for which running water is symbolic of strength and life.

Water is central. It flows in clearly delineated runs that are far from straight, but which meander along, or it pools in ponds that are clearly set apart from the surrounding area. Gravel and stones are important design features. Marginal and aquatic plants are placed carefully, but used singly as a focal point.

MEDITERRANEAN GARDENS

Mediterranean-style gardens are modeled on those of Italy. Paving and walls are kept in warm, earthy tones, with terracotta pots and containers exercising a decisive influence on the garden's appearance. Water pouring from an amphora into an ornamental pool complements this style perfectly, and a swimming pool is also likely to be top of the list here.

MODERN GARDENS

The image of the modern garden is determined by design artifacts and contemporary materials such as stainless steel and high quality artificial substances that are mostly all one shade. In planting, particular attention is paid to clear lines and themes on a single color.

Areas of water separated with a strong border are thus highly recommended. A formal ornamental pool in a geometric shape, or a water course with straight lines, fits in perfectly. In smaller gardens, spheres with water bubbling out of them are an attractive feature.

Wild gardens

The objective here is planting with native species that are most appropriate to Nature, and therefore ecologically sound. The plants should be able to establish themselves without too much horticultural intervention. In so doing the design itself takes second place to the living and growing conditions of flora and fauna.

Water feature design should also comply with these principles. Naturalistic water courses and pools that blend inconspicuously into the overall design emphasize the horticultural intent behind this type of garden. It is not so much the surface of the water that is emphasized, but the planting in and around the water with native bog and aquatic plants.

ROCKERIES

The most important design element is stones of different sizes, especially on sloping sites. They are scattered around the garden loosely and naturalistically on different levels and planted with appropriate rock garden species and shrubs.

On sloping sites it is therefore worth incorporating natural-looking water courses into the rockery. Water emerging from between two upright rocks of different sizes creates a pleasing effect; the end of the water course should be marked by a natural-looking gravel pool where the water collects.

A RECREATIONAL RESOURCE

What could be more refreshing on a hot summer's day that tumbling into the cool water of a pool? What epitomizes that holiday feeling more than drifting on an inflatable in a bathing pond? What could be more fun for children playing in the garden than damming a water course and floating homemade boats? Water in the garden can be so much more than a design feature or a habitat for flora and fauna: it can be a hobby and recreational resource for you, your family, and your friends.

SWIMMING POOLS

For decades a swimming pool in the garden was the last word in luxury and extravagance, but nowadays it has to share this status with the bathing pond. In contrast to the latter, though, the swimming pool offers the advantage of clear water and thus unclouded bathing pleasure in every sense of the word. It comes at a price, though—an expensive filtration and treatment plant and a high level of maintenance on the one hand, and ecologically damaging water additives on the other.

BATHING PONDS

They blend harmoniously into the overall garden design, guarantee enjoyable bathing and are not so harmful to Nature. They are not to every taste, though, and anyone considering installing a bathing pond should ask themselves whether bathing in a pool without a solid bed, and which contains plants and animals, will be a problem.

The aim of a bathing pond is not just to create a visually attractive aquatic recreational area, but above all to ensure that the water cleans itself naturally, without chemical additives, as far as possible.

Thus there is always a purification area attached to the actual bathing pond. The composition of its floor and appropriate planting ensure that harmful substances are filtered out of the

water. In appearance and layout this area is like a natural-looking garden pond.

The size of the purification zone must correspond roughly to the size of the bathing pond in order for underwater plants and floating leaved plants, grasses, reeds and so on to thoroughly clear the water. This means that you need a lot of space for a bathing pond: there is little sense in creating one if you have less than 130 sq ft (40 sq m) available.

The purification zone need not necessarily be located right next to the bathing area; it can be some distance away and be linked to the bathing pond by a water course or overflow. Creating a bathing pond requires expert knowledge, unlike a garden pond, which you can create in the garden yourself using basic manual skills. It is better to entrust installation of a bathing pond to a specialist company.

All in all, installing a bathing pond is just as expensive a pleasure as a swimming pool. You not only need to be swimming in it, you also need plenty of land.

Garden paddling pools and showers

More reasonably priced and also suitable for use in small gardens, garden paddling pools are only erected during the summer months. They may not offer the comfort of a swimming pool or bathing pond but, despite the smaller area of water, there's no shortage of fun, especially for children, who are usually more than satisfied with such a pool.

A shower or a sprinkler device attached to the garden hose is another extremely cheap alternative for water play outdoors. The best place to put one up is on a lawn, where the water can drain away easily.

The Garden Pond

TRANQUIL BEAUTY

The idea of a garden that incorporates water necessarily evokes the concept of a garden pond, because ponds are the most versatile way to enhance garden design. A garden pond is a beautiful oasis of tranquility that provides fascinating habitat for a unique flora and fauna.

In addition, by a garden pond is the best place to relax. It appeals to the senses on many levels. The surface of the water, usually only slightly ruffled, provides a wonderful, impressionistic reflection of the sky, clouds, and tree canopy. Depending on the time of day, and season, the light dances on the water in myriad reflections, and plants with floating leaves, above all the various types of water lily, beguile the senses with utterly beautiful blooms.

The tranquil water invites relaxation and inspiration, diffuses refreshing coolness, and lets you get closer to Nature. The surface of a garden pond reflects the changing seasons in a way that no other garden design feature can—a frozen pond in winter, mist over the water in spring, reduced water levels in summer, and the wind rippling the surface of the water in the fall. Take a closer look for even more detailed insights, such as the changing shades in the water as the seasons turn.

POND STYLES

The choices for garden pond design are limitless—ultimately every pond site is a distinctive, unique specimen. Here is a summary of the main types of ponds.

THE NATURALISTIC POND

The most popular form of garden pond is the naturalistic one. The organically shaped, rounded banks blend harmoniously into the garden. The transition between water and land is gentle —scarcely perceptible thanks to a carefully designed marginal area.

In addition to the basic structure and the fine tuning of the pond margins, it is mainly the choice of plants that is important. You will create the desired impression only when the pond planting merges seamlessly from the bog and marginal areas to the rest of the garden. You'll achieve this by choosing the plants carefully to blend with each other. A naturalistic pond does not happen naturally—it needs a little help.

THE WILD POND

Quite the opposite is true of what is known as a wild pond. Here Nature is left almost completely to her own devices, to provide a unique refuge for native plants and animals. The pond itself is of secondary importance; the flora and fauna create, and thus also design, their own habitats.

The result is a biotype that is not entirely devoid of human intervention. Over time a wild pond will silt up, so the bottom must be dredged regularly. Also, in the end you will not be able to avoid thinning out rapidly spreading plants.

THE GRAVEL-BOTTOMED POND

The floor of the pond is not covered in substrate but in gravel and pebbles of different sizes, and perhaps different colors too. Rounded natural stones also dominate the pond's border. Thanks to this covering of gravel the bottom of the pool looks clean, and therefore fits well into formal gardens.

THE FOREST POOL

Sited mainly in the shade—cool, refreshing, and romantic—that's the image we have of a pool at the heart of a big stand of trees. Because many aquatic plants are sun lovers, there is only a limited range of plants that can be grown. Different ferns and grasses do very well though, around the water's edge. A black pond liner fits in well with the pool's appearance.

THE ORNAMENTAL POND

In contrast to all the types of pond mentioned previously, here there is no attempt to make the body of water look natural. Quite the opposite: the ornamental pond, also known as a formal pond, is obviously an intentionally arranged design feature.

The pond's basic form is no longer restricted to the rounded and organic. Any shape is possible and thus there is the option of mirroring the lines of the house with a rectangular pond. Circular shapes and combinations of strictly formal and natural-seeming pond borders are equally possible.

Pond border design is not limited any more to natural stone or soil, either. You can take your pick of materials and choose

those in keeping with your garden's overall design. Sawn timber is the most popular choice, whether in the form of planks, as a palisade, or something different. The pond edging is just as likely to be in worked natural stone as industrially manufactured tiles.

When a pond borders directly onto a patio and the same material used to create the pond surrounds and paves the patio, the finished look is especially harmonious.

In addition, the pond need no longer be on the same level as the garden; the basin can be raised up so it stands out from the surrounding area, making the details more eye catching. There are no hard and fast design rules about how to clad the sides of the pond.

SITING PONDS

Anyone thinking of installing a pond has more to bear in mind than just the type of pond and the look they want to create. A whole range of other factors must be taken into consideration in order to achieve an enduringly beautiful garden pond that functions perfectly as a habitat and requires little in the way of upkeep.

CHOICE OF LOCATION AND SIZE

The most important decision concerns location. The key question is the pond's importance as a design feature. Should it be the most important element in the garden's design, or just one of many features? The question not only relates to the size of the pond, but also where it is positioned within the garden. A pond at the back of the garden, for example, is not as immediately striking as a stretch of water right next to the patio.

How the neighboring garden segments are planted is also important for the overall visual impact. If the pond is located in the middle of a lawn, for example, it draws the eye much more when it is not surrounded by tall plants.

When laying out the pond, remember that the area of visible water in the finished pond does not correspond to the pond's original shape and size. For one thing, the plants take up part of the surface area, especially in the bog and shallow areas;

for another, the water level is not usually on a par with the ground level, but about 4 in (10 cm) below it. The banks slope gently away too, so the resulting optical illusion means that the water surface looks smaller. The pond's appearance also changes throughout the year as the plants grow.

The bigger the plants in the bog area and shallows become, the further they extend over the water's surface. Plants that increase in height also reduce the overall view of the sur-

RATIOS OF SCALE

If the pond is to be incorporated into the garden as an interesting but not overpowering garden feature, the rule of thumb is that it should not occupy more than one-seventh of the available space. If the body of water takes up much more space than this, then the pond becomes the most important design feature in the garden.

face. Water lilies or other floating plants cover a part of it, so the contrast between water and marginal planting is reduced. All this leads to the pond looking smaller than it actually is.

Where size is concerned, it is also worth bearing in mind whether you intend to have fish in the pond at a later date. Most fish need water at least 2 ft 6 in (80 cm) deep and plenty of room to swim. For many other pond inhabitants, such as salamanders

and frogs, it is important that they have sufficiently large bog areas and shallows.

Last, but not least, your own ideas on how you will use the pond are critical for your choice of site. If, for example, first and foremost you want to relax by the pond, locate it next to the patio or a lawn that will be used as a seating area.

If, on the other hand, you intend your pond to be a refuge for fauna and flora, it would be better positioned in a quieter, more remote part of the garden. Sunshine is especially important for acclimating and growing plants; many of them, especially floating plants and shrubs, like warm, bright conditions. Others, though, such as ferns, flourish better in shadier areas.

Ideally, during the day, there should always be some part of the pond that is in

shade, but it should be possible to grow most of the plants in a sunny position. A site in partial shade also helps the ecological balance in the water (see p. 88).

Ponds are heavy on maintenance, not just because the surface of the water has to be cleaned regularly, but also because the plants need to be pruned or thinned out.

When planning your pond make sure it is easily accessible and that you can reach all the planting areas easily. Ideally it should be accessible all the way round, with the extent of the water being such that the entire surface can be reached, and cleaned, with a long scoop.

The amount of maintenance a pond needs is largely dependent upon its ecological balance. As a rule of thumb, the bigger the pond, the quicker it becomes self-cleaning and so requires less maintenance. A decisive factor is the care with which the plants have been chosen for their compatibility with each other and with the type of water. Optimum conditions are achieved when the total bog and shallow water areas that are so important for regeneration take up as much space as the areas of deep water.

Other requirements

In the case of almost every pond, when drawing up the basic plans you need to consider technical matters. You have to think about a power supply for electrical features such as pumps and lights. In the case of larger ponds you need to allow for more comprehensive technology, such as a filtration plant.

Safety

When planning your pond you should always bear safety in mind, especially where young children are concerned. A pond always represents a potential source of danger to them. Even if there are no children in your family, access to the pond or your property must be secured so that other people's children cannot stray near the water. If there is the possibility of young children getting to the pond, then it absolutely must be fenced off with a sufficiently high barrier.

An important factor that should not be underestimated is excavating the pond. Removing several cubic yards (meters) of earth is expensive and should be taken into consideration in the early planning stages. The best solution is to incorporate the soil into the basic garden design. Thus the soil can be used to make a hill for a water course to run down.

LAYING OUT PONDS

There are two alternatives available when laying out a pond: using pre-formed liners or designing your own layout using a liner that you cut to size. Each has its advantages and disadvantages.

Pre-formed ponds

The easiest way to build your pond is by using a pre-formed liner. These are only suitable for smaller ponds with a maximum length of around 13 ft (4 m).

These liners are available commercially in a wide range of shapes and sizes. The edge of the liner is shaped to allow for bog and shallow water areas, so they are relatively easy to plant up. Larger liners come with pre-formed inserts for filters or pumps.

If the liner is fitted properly in the ground and the aquatic planting and marginal planting designs are appropriate, the overall result can be very pleasing. When the plants have matured, these ponds can look completely natural.

On the down side, the design options are very limited. The shape is predetermined by the manufacturer—customized designs are not possible. Also, pre-formed liners are much more expensive than conventional pond liners, but you recoup some of this additional expense in the labor you save, and using these off-the-shelf products reduces to a minimum the risk of making major mistakes when laying out your pond.

Pre-formed ponds are made from two types of material: the smaller liners usually from polyethylene (PE), and the bigger ones from fiberglass reinforced plastic (FRP). Both materials have similar properties:

- LIFESPAN (branded manufacturers guarantee them for up to 15 years)

- NONTOXIC CONSTRUCTION (fish friendly)

- UV AND FROST RESISTANT

- HIGH DEGREE OF RESISTANCE TO TEARS (high resistance to penetration by plants roots)

Basically it can be said that it is worth buying branded products. Not only are they guaranteed for up to 15 years, the manufacturers also sell suitable accessories.

As far as size is concerned, generally the wider and longer the pond, the deeper it should be. The smallest ponds are about 3 sq ft (1 sq m) and 16 in (40 cm) deep. The largest have a surface area of around 30 sq ft (10 sq m), with a maximum depth of around 3 ft (1 m).

Precise dimensions are not possible, though, because the liners are shaped differently. To compare the different sizes, it's better to look at the capacity in gallons (or liters), rather than the dimensions in feet (or meters). They range from around 33 to 880 gal (150 to 4000 l).

CONVENTIONAL LINERS

The advantage of conventional liners is that your pond can be designed to suit the exact individual requirements of your garden. Also, with this material there's no problem in accommodating large scale pond designs. Your design is not restricted in any way.

Using conventional liners has its disadvantages too, though: building a pond with them not only entails a lot more planning, but is also more complicated, and this applies to all three stages of the operation:

DECIDING THE BASIC SHAPE: In contrast to pre-formed liners, when using a conventional liner you have to think very carefully about the pond levels, because it will be possible to plant up the margins only if you terrace the pond.

BUILDING THE POND: The pond must be constructed with great care: it is most important to prevent the liner from leaking. Carefully remove any stones and roots from the hole, then apply a layer of sand and a layer of felt to cushion the actual liner. The liner is put down last of all. There's a choice of standard liner materials, such as PVC, or rubber liners that are manufactured using more environmentally friendly methods.

MARGIN DESIGN: Finally, the pond margins must be individually planned and executed, the main concern being to prevent the water being soaked up by the surrounding soil as a result of capillarity.

The water course

INHERENTLY APPEALING

A garden water course is not necessarily a natural feature, but irrespective of whether it meanders slowly through a meadow, splashes gently over stones, or pours unchecked down a gradient, moving water's diverse facets speak to several senses simultaneously.

The eye is caught by the dancing reflections, and the calming splash of water reaches the ear. Particularly in summer, if you are right next to water you experience Nature's special aromas and feel refreshing coolness.

Even if the water in your garden only meanders a few feet through the greenery and hardly reflects the whole spectrum of experiences provided by a natural water course, the significant impressions and effects that even the smallest water course contributes can permanently enrich your garden design.

Water courses that imitate Nature speak directly to the senses, not just because their unmistakable appearance immediately attracts the eye, but also because the water's movement, when it catches the light in such a fascinating way and reflects the immediate surroundings in rippling reflections, is also a visual treat.

The plants that make their homes at the side of a stream are intriguing for everyone, not just gardeners. Many plants love the moist soil conditions on either side of a water course. Grasses and ferns, for example, find ideal living conditions here and display especially deep shades of green right beside the water.

Where the sun penetrates right through to the stream bed, perennials and ground cover plants put on a lavish display of blooms. The image of the luxuriant plant growth contrasts with the stony stream bed whose intensified colors glitter through the water.

A NATURAL EXPERIENCE

Most of all, relaxing in the garden creates a special link to Nature in which the gentle background murmuring or splashing of a stream can make a major contribution. In fact, people tend to find total silence uncomfortable—the delicate, natural harmony of a stream pervades this silence, so the relaxation value of a water course, at least as far as hearing is concerned, is especially high.

Nature lovers will find that a garden stream is an interesting area for discovery. Mini-beasts and insects in particular are attracted to the environment of a wild stream. Certain species of dragonfly, for example, or even frogs, are just as much at home here as they are in a pond. In addition, birds flock to use areas of standing water or shallows as drinking stations.

TYPES OF SOIL

Of course you need a suitable gradient for a water course, otherwise the water will not flow. Depending on the gradient and the
shape, there are three basic types of water courses suitable for
garden design: the meadow stream, the mountain stream, and
the formal water course.

THE MEADOW STREAM

Here the water flows very slowly through an almost flat terrain.
The stream has an atmosphere of great peacefulness and weaves
gently through the garden. The gradient for a meadow stream is
one to two percent. By creating large dammed areas, it's possible
to construct a stream that is a good 30 ft (10 m) long, with a dif-
ference in height of no more than 4 to 8 in (10 to 20 cm) along its
entire length.

Thanks to the low flow rate, this type of water course offers perfect conditions for all kinds of bog and some aquatic plants. In principle such an arrangement consists of lining up a series of several narrow, elongated mini-ponds, where the water flows visibly in only a few places, and moves imperceptibly from one dam level to the next. This is why there is water in each section of stream, without the use of a pump, at almost any given time.

The disadvantage, on the other hand, is that it is hardly possible to see the water move. The stream does not have a dynamic effect, and there is little to listen to, because the water slips silently over low dam levels.

THE MOUNTAIN STREAM

The opposite can be said of the mountain stream. Here the water moves through the garden dynamically thanks to a larger gradient. It flows over dams up to 12 in (30 cm) high. In some places proper waterfalls may even form. The visibly moving current rushes loudly over stones to the next section of stream.

Reflections in the water show up especially well; as a design feature the stream is to the fore not only acoustically, but also visually.

To lay out such a water course in the garden you need a much steeper gradient than for a meadow stream. You will

only get the desired effect with an overall gradient of 10 to 15 percent, so a mountain stream is especially suitable for sloping sites.

You can also create the necessary height on flatter sites with just a little landscaping. You don't even need much space. Because of its greater visual and acoustic presence, you need a much shorter bed than for a meadow stream to achieve an effective mountain stream.

One attractive solution is to create a mound of earth 3 to 5 ft (1 to 1.5 m) high and to contain this hill with large chunks

of rock. The hill need only be about 6 ft (2 m) wide. Install a pond immediately in front of this mound, and lay out the mountain stream bed down a relatively steeply sloping part of it.

The downside to a mountain stream is that it will only look attractive if the water is flowing all the time. If the pump is switched off, then the appeal will have vanished.

The steeper the gradient between stream and pool, the more water will flow into it. This means that the pumps that transport the water back from the pool to the head of the stream must be more powerful than would be necessary for a less steep drop. This takes a lot of electricity and is tough on the environment, and your wallet.

Finally, a very steep stream does not provide the optimum living conditions for aquatic and bog plants, which get washed away if the flow rate is too fast. Thus, plants are restricted to small areas of still water or dams.

THE FORMAL WATER COURSE

The third recommended design option is the formal water course, which relies less on the course of Nature. It is more suitable for emphasizing an overall design concept for the garden.

Above all, the aesthetic impact of ornamental ponds can be heightened by formally designed water courses, most of all by several stepped basins, where the water flows visibly and audibly from one to the next. To achieve this, three rectangular basins are often arranged in a tier, with each separate basin not only acting as a little pool in its own right, but also as a cascade. To keep the water flowing, a closed water circuit is installed using a pump and appropriate pipes.

The transition to a stream can thus "flow" in every sense of the word; in modern garden architecture in particular, the water moves from smaller to larger basins and then runs through a narrow, straight water course. Natural stone is the preferred design material, although formal water courses of this kind can also be obtained in pre-formed materials such as brick, to blend specifically with the architecture of the house.

LAYING WATER COURSES

There are three different ways of laying a water course: water course shells, pond liner, and compressed concrete.

■ WATER COURSE SHELLS: The simplest way to lay out a water course is to use commercially available water course shells. Different, pre-formed units are placed in series, or staggered, to create the water course. The units, between 20 in and 3 ft (50 and 100 cm) long, are available in various shapes such as spring section, bend section, or end section. Immediately after installation the water course looks unattractive and very artificial, but this changes when the banks are planted up and the growth partly covers the shells. Individual, naturalistic design is not, however, possible with water course shells.

■ POND LINER: If you want your water course to integrate fully into your garden and look as natural as possible, and if you value individuality, then you should use pond liner to build it. The process is a similar one to building a pond (see p. 46). Excavate the water course, spread sand or felt to protect the liner, lay out the liner, and create a natural look using gravel and stones.

Lining a stream bed entails a great deal more work than using pre-formed

shells, although the materials are not quite as expensive, and the finished look is much more convincing.

- COMPRESSED CONCRETE: Instead of using pond liner you can resort to compressed concrete, but this only makes sense if you're laying a large-scale water course. In this case you need to work out the shape accurately, because it can't be changed later.

You will therefore have to decide in advance the position of the bigger stones, for example, which should ultimately look like they got in the stream bed by chance, and produce a corresponding mould in compressed concrete.

Miniature water paradise

WATER FEATURES, MINI-PONDS IN CONTAINERS, ETC.

If you want to incorporate water into your garden as an attractive design feature, you needn't install a large pond or a long water course. One of the advantages of water is that it enhances a garden just as much when used on a small scale.

Once again, the options are multiple: from a simple bowl filled with water, or a little bird bath, to artfully designed water spouts and imaginative water features, a veritable treasure trove of mini-ponds made from containers, stones with water bubbling out of them, fountains, and springs.

Of course, these smaller water features can't compare with their bigger conterparts in every respect, but they can still be beneficial. A stone with water bubbling out of it conveys splashing water just as well as a water course, and beautifully designed water features are just as eye-catching as a big pond.

There is one reservation, though: the opportunities for growing aquatic and bog plants are very few. Most of these plants need much more space to develop than a pond in a container can offer.

BOWLS AND TROUGHS

You need neither a big garden nor a lot of financial resources for a bowl filled with blossoms, or a little bird bath. Even a balcony has room for them.

And even if they appear very small and unassuming, that is precisely their attraction, because they are testament to a lovingly designed recreational space in the open air.

They are shown off to especially good advantage if they don't leap right out at you, but are tucked away to catch a lazily

wandering eye, a miniature water feature on a side table, for example, concealed amongst ground cover plants, or set into a bed of flowering perennials.

MINI-PONDS IN CONTAINERS

There are multiple variations available on the theme of small-scale water features: tubs and barrels, stucco troughs and wheel-barrows, hollowed out tree trunks or wooden crates, industrially manufactured clay pots or sheet steel tubs. In fact, any kind of container that holds water, and that provides a large, visible surface, is suitable.

The container does not even have to be watertight—a rotten barrel or a nice, big tub that has split its seams is simply fitted with a pond liner to make it suitable. You only need a liner that is 0.02 in (0.5 mm) thick. The container is lined loosely throughout, with the liner either folded over or glued to the inside at the top, or tacked down, as appropriate.

Space is at a premium, and this applies equally when planting up mini-ponds. Of course, they won't provide a home for botanical giants – but a whole range of little floating plants that don't need to root in soil, such as water cress (*Pistia stratiotes*) or water hyacinth (*Eichhornia crassipes*), both of which are tender, are happy with an inch or so (a couple of centimeters) of water.

Small varieties of water lily, especially dwarf water lilies (*Nymphaea pygmaea*) are eye catching. Of bog plants that root in soil and only need to be covered by an inch or so of water, there

are attractive dwarf varieties such as water plantain (*Alisma plantago-aquatica*) or beardless iris (*Iris laevigata*).

With a little horticultural skill and/or appropriate advice from a specialist supplier, it is relatively easy to conjure up an attractive group of plants. Graded planting looks especially effective here, with tall flowering plants at the back, e.g. pickerel weed (*Pontederia cordata*) or flowering rush (*Buromus umbellatus*), little floating plants on the water, such as frogbit (*Hydrocharis morsusranae*) or water hyacinth (*Eichornia crassipes*), and little plants at the front, such as parrot feather water milfoil (*Myriophyllum aquaticum*) or marsh violet (*Viola palustris*).

If you use several containers of the same type, but not necessarily the same size, grouped together or tiered, this opens up a mass of versatile design opportunities. If they are then planted up differently, the result is especially pleasing.

Since mini-ponds should not be filled with water over winter, or should be moved to a frost-free position, your container pond is also the perfect place to grow imported beauties that are not hardy, such as kaffir lilies (*Schizostylis coccinea*) or cardinal flower (*Lobelia fulgens*). Since most little plants suitable for a container pond are sun-lovers, it's best to choose a sunny position.

Unlike most other water features, the list of materials for container ponds is almost endless, but most have specific advantages and disadvantages.

- WOOD: On the one hand, wood and water being both natural materials, they work especially well together but, on the other, nothing is worse for wood than being permanently soaked. The wood can be impregnated only when there's no question of it coming into contact with the pond water, otherwise the water will be contaminated by the chemical compounds released over time. This is why we recommend first thoroughly impregnating wooden containers, especially made from soft woods like pine or deal, and then lining them with thin pond liner.

- PLASTIC: There's virtually no cheaper and easier way to create a container pond than by filling a big planter tub or stucco trough with water. Not just because the material is inexpensive, but because this kind of mini-pond does not even have to be made watertight. There's only one little problem – the containers aren't always pleasing to look at.

The art, therefore, lies in either concealing the unsightly container completely, or at least making it blend into the background. In addition to the low cost versions of containers used for purposes other than originally intended, higher quality alternatives such as plastic, ceramic or stoneware imitations, are available commercially too.

- CERAMIC AND EARTHENWARE: Beautiful and classic on the one hand, expensive and fragile on the other. These are the main characteristics of the ceramic and earthenware containers available commercially, especially those for creating container ponds. It is worth remembering that the more lavishly the fired containers are decorated, the more expensive they will be. Bear in mind that most containers are not frost proof. Even if stickers on the pots claim otherwise, we still recommend that you empty out the water before the first frost. The frost-proof aspect applies to the material only, if at all; only in exceptional cases do these expensive containers allow for the stresses imposed by a freezing body of water.

- ZINC AND SHEET STEEL: A tin bath, or a special container for ponds made from coated sheet steel, is also an attractive way to house a mini-pond. You should ensure that the alloys will not pollute the water. Tin baths and containers that are not made with specially treated sheet steel should also be lined with a pond liner.

STONE TROUGHS

Once they were used to water cattle or horses, but today they number among the romantic representatives of water garden design in a small space. Since it is now very rare to find a genuinely old stone trough, numerous manufacturers have included industrially produced troughs in their product ranges. There are basically three types:

BASIC TROUGH: A solid basin made from natural or artificial stone, rectangular shaped and in various sizes, is the closest to the typical image of a trough. The stone basin has an overflow, but not an integrated inlet. It is fed by an external water source such as a spring or pump.

TROUGH WITH PUMP: A hand pump is attached to the trough, although it is not used as it was originally. It's more a decorative feature and is used for the water supply. An electric pump ensures that water flows permanently from the pump into the basin via a closed circuit, thus creating the pleasant acoustic impression of constantly running water.

TROUGH WITH PLANTING AREA: In this case the trough's length is divided in two: water flows into one basin from a linked hand pump with electric water circulation, and the second basin serves as a planting area.

Troughs made up of a smaller and a larger basin are also available commercially. They can thus be tiered, for example, and used alternately for water or plants.

In theory it is possible to plant up the water basin, but only if water does not flow into it all the time. The water movement is too great for the small area, so aquatic plants would not find it a favorable habitat.

SOURCE STONES AND WATER SPOUTS

The spring reminds us of rebirth, and it accordingly exerts a primal fascination. Water appearing to spring straight from the depths of the Earth is thus a popular design feature in water gardening. It not only pleases the eyes, but also the ears, with its splashing sound.

There are two different options worth considering in a small garden: the source stone and the water spout. Basically both require a closed water circuit; the water that flows from the spring must be collected and fed back to the spring via a circulation pump.

We talk about a "source stone" when the water bubbles out of a single water feature and, although the name suggests it, the material used need not necessarily be natural stone. For example, a terracotta amphora lying on its side, or a mass-produced product in an artificial material, can act equally well as a source stone.

Water that visibly bubbles over is particularly attractive: this is true of all kinds of springs. The water should spurt up out of the hole to a height of about 2 in (5 cm). The pump must be precisely adjusted to achieve this effect. The simplest option is to

buy an off-the-shelf kit that includes a suitable pump. Industrially manufactured features even have a recess underneath, where the pump can be installed invisibly.

Although there are infinite possibilities for making water bubble up out of somewhere or something, there are certain kinds of springs and water spouts that are especially popular:

ERRATICS: The water bubbles up out of an "erratic," a large round stone. To achieve this, a natural or artificial stone has a vertical hole drilled, so that a water pipe can be fed up through it from beneath. Complete kits are available commercially.

Alternatively, a small trough is hollowed out as a reservoir and fitted with pond liner. In order to introduce the water supply easily underneath the source stone, the collection basin created is covered with large pebbles (diameter 1 to 2 in / 3 to 5 cm). The source stone is placed on top of the pebbles and the pump is housed in, or close to, the reservoir.

MILLSTONES: This kind of source stone design is available commercially in artificial stone, with different diameters and strengths. In contrast to genuine millstones, mass-produced copies have the advantage of the central hole being tailored to their role as a water feature, so they are simple to install and operate.

SPHERES: Colorful balls with a hole in them where the water bubbles out are extremely popular. One reason for this must surely be that they integrate well into any garden style; there's a suitable feature of this kind for all gardens, from small, romantic cottage plots, to highly designed expanses.

Spheres are available commercially in a multitude of materials, colors, and surfaces. The spectrum ranges from mechanically finished, smooth, shiny blue ceramic balls, to hand-crafted, artfully decorated natural stone spheres. For garden use the most suitable are large balls with diameters exceeding 12 in (30 cm); smaller balls are recommended

only for ponds in containers or interior design. Used singly, the balls are placed on a special concealing platform, which hides the water supply mechanics. The water collects here, and is also pumped from here back up to the top. To increase the visual impact, after it has been positioned in the garden, the platform should be invisible; the best way to conceal it is with fine gravel.

AMPHORAE: The models for this special type of water feature are found all around the Mediterranean. Accordingly, these reclining terracotta jars, out of which the water pours as if by accident, are best suited to a Mediterranean-style garden. Amphorae are available in various sizes, but when making your purchase ensure that it is frost proof.

■ CLASSIC WATER SPOUTS: Whether it's an animal spout, a cute figure of a boy relieving himself, or a spouting head, there are many selections on offer. They combine equally well with an ornamental pond or pond in a container.

SOURCE STONES AND WATER SPOUTS

Fountains in the garden are attractive, extremely useful, and highly symbolic. It's no longer necessary to dig into the ground; on the contrary, all you have to do is install a moderately deep basin, which can be fitted out as a fountain.

Where water gardening technology is concerned, there are two options. On the one hand, the fountain can be designed as a purely decorative feature with a closed water circuit. It can also, on the other, be equipped with a fixed supply and an appropriate outlet so that, as a consequence, the fountain has a highly practical use – for filling watering cans or cleaning garden tools.

BASIC DESIGN

There are two basic versions where design is concerned. A retaining wall with pre-shaped stones is cheap and relatively easy to implement. Basins hewn from natural stone are much more expensive, but also look more exclusive. The visual effect is determined by the water supply design in conjunction with the basic shape of the actual fountain. Depending on the type of garden and your personal taste, there is a choice of different versions, from a simple water faucet to an artistically designed supply pipe.

Connection to a water butt

Connecting your fountain to a water butt is highly recommended from the ecological point of view and money-saving in the long term. The water butt is half buried and surrounded by stones. The fountain has two water supplies—an invisible one coming from the water butt and an adjustable, visible tap water supply. This can thus be used as necessary, or the water level can be kept constant during a dry period.

A pump can be connected for watering the garden; otherwise simply scoop water from the fountain with a watering can. It is important to install an overflow, which will prevent flooding after heavy rainfall.

Water quality

BIOLOGICAL BALANCE

Irrespective of the water feature you choose for your garden, the water must always be of a certain quality in order to provide flora and fauna with a healthy habitat.

If the water quality is poor, plants and fish die. One of the most important objectives in gardening with water should be consistently ideal water quality that is as natural as possible, and is maintained with little effort. Water quality is always directly related to planting, microorganisms, and the animal kingdom. It

is dependent upon planning the body of water from the outset, so that a balance can be established. This means that natural factors, mainly plants and animals, have the job of maintaining water quality.

This undertaking can be illustrated using the example of populating a garden pond with fish. On the one hand, fish eat certain aquatic plants, helping to keep their spread under control. This helps maintain the ecological balance.

On the other hand, fish utilize oxygen to survive; the pond's oxygen content is reduced, which in turn has a detrimental effect on water quality. Fish also pollute the water.

So, populating a garden pond with fish has its advantages and disadvantages for the biological balance.

The same applies to aquatic plants. Water quality is primarily determined by its plant nutrient content. If the pond becomes overfertilized with too many plants, or the wrong plants, or if it does not receive enough attention, then the water quality will deteriorate.

Plants, on the other hand, are important oxygenators and are thus of inestimable value to the ecological balance.

THE KEY FACTORS

Water quality is determined by various factors, primarily the degree of hardness, pH value, and oxygen and nutrient content. Water temperature is also decisive.

DEGREE OF HARDNESS

One of the most important values relates to the mineral salts contained in the water. The mineral content is described as differing degrees of hardness. The unit of measurement for this is general hardness (GH).

We differentiate between three degrees of hardness in relation to domestic water supply from local water companies, which are given in ppm (parts per million)or dH (degrees of hardness):

■ SOFT WATER: 70 to 140 ppm / 4 to 8 dH

■ MEDIUM HARD WATER: 140 to 320 ppm / 8 to 17 dH

■ HARD WATER: 320 to 530 ppm / 18 to 30 dH

Garden pond plants and animals require medium hard water for optimum development. If the water falls much below 175 ppm / 10 dH, or rises much above 350 ppm / 20 dH, then

you need to intervene. Rainwater and spring water are usually quite soft. If the pond is mainly fed by such water, or if heavy rainfall leads to the degree of hardness falling, then the degree of hardness can be increased by special additives available from dealers, thus stabilizing the water quality.

pH VALUE

The next big target is the degree of acidity in the water. It is defined by the pH value, which expresses the sum of the acids and alkalis dissolved in the water.

As with water hardness, there are three categories:

▬ ACIDIC WATER: pH value 0 to 6.9

▬ NEUTRAL WATER: pH value 7

▬ ALKALINE WATER: pH value 7.1 to 14

Concentrations of acids that are too high are just as harmful to aquatic plants and animals as excessive concentrations of alkalis. Most ornamental fish in a garden pond can survive only at pH values between 6 and 9, for example, and they are happiest with pH values between 7 and 8. If the values are not met or are exceeded, various diseases can develop, such as those of the skin, gills, or fins.

No pond has a constant pH value. It can drop, especially after heavy rain. Additionally, leaves floating and rotting on the water's surface in fall can have a lasting impact on pH value. Commercial additives to regulate the water's pH value are available from specialists. A simpler and cheaper alternative, though, is to replace some of the pond water.

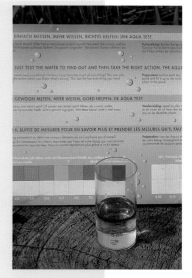

Testing water quality

A wide range of water analysis kits are available commercially. They not only determine the GH value and thus the calcium oxide content, but also the proportion of carbonates present in the water, which is measured in KH, for carbonate hardness. Recommended carbonate values are in the region of 50 to 175 ppm / 3 to10 dH. It is also possible, with these kits, to determine pH values and nitrate content.

OXYGEN

Plants and animals in the water also need oxygen, so the pond water must contain sufficient quantities at any given time. Water is basically supplied with oxygen by movement and by photosynthesis.

▬ WATER MOVEMENT: The most effective form of oxygen supply. As a result of contact with, and agitation by, the air, the water takes up part of the oxygen content. Where running water is concerned, oxygen deficiency is rarely a problem. In the case of standing garden ponds, however, oxygen deficiency can occur easily, especially in areas of deeper water where the water does not come into contact with the air.

Even a gentle breeze agitates the water. The wind can be prevented from reaching the pond as a result of design faults. This may be the case, for example, if the pond site is sheltered from the wind. Contact with the air is also prevented by a preponderance of plants with floating leaves.

A simple method of avoiding oxygen deficiency is to circulate the water. Special commercial aeration pumps are available, but including a spring or water course in your pond design is just as effective.

▬ PHOTOSYNTHESIS: Like plants that grow in soil, aquatic plants also produce oxygen. This process, called photosynthesis or assimilation, requires light as an energy source. Carefully chosen underwater plants are the best means of increasing the proportion of oxygen in the water.

Plants in their turn need oxygen, although a whole group of them, such as algae, need even more than they give off. Keeping a pond free of excess algae is therefore important not only for aesthetic reasons; first and foremost, it assists with water quality too.

In addition to plants, it is mainly fish that constantly remove oxygen from the water. Too many fish in a pond and they rob each other of their means of existence, especially in summer, when organic decomposition processes that consume oxygen proceed more quickly than in winter.

Dying plants are also great consumers of oxygen since decomposition requires vast quantities. There is thus an urgent need to remove leaves or other dead plant material that float on the water as quickly and thoroughly as possible.

NUTRIENT CONTENT

Water constantly deposits organic materials, be they plant material, fish waste, or food residues. Nitrogen compounds, primarily nitrates, are produced as a result of a complex chemical process.

Most aquatic plants use this nitrate as a nutrient, i.e. it acts as a fertilizer. But if the water's nitrate content rises too quickly, there is an explosion in algae growth, and the balance goes haywire. The nitrate content should not, therefore, be too high, the optimum level being less than 25 milligrams per liter (mg/l), but from 50 milligrams/liter the situation becomes critical.

The simplest way to counteract an excessive concentration of nutrients is to introduce aquatic plants that are nutrient hungry. In addition, it is worth avoiding excessive pollution by cleaning the water regularly and caring for your pond, as well as not overfeeding your fish.

If there are raised concentrations of nitrogen in your water, then you will need biological additives to provide emergency help. In the long term, though, further concentration should be avoided by making sure you have appropriate plants.

TEMPERATURE

The environmental temperature is just as important for aquatic plants as it is for those on land. In the same way that plants sprout, burst into life, and blossom in spring, the vitality of water plants is also associated with warmth.

Thus, aquatic plants grow much more quickly in warmer water than cold, and they also spread more quickly. The water should not be too warm considering the fish, though; fish have very different sensitivities to high water temperatures.

If it is too warm—primarily due to strong sunlight—you may be presented with another problem: water evaporation. In the worst case this progresses to the point where the water dries up altogether, and the plants and fish die.

Conversely, temperatures that are too low can also be very problematic. Frost not only damages many exotic aquatic plants that are not winter hardy, but a thick layer of ice on the pond prevents many species of fish from breathing.

It is therefore worth keeping an eye on the water and the environmental temperature, especially in winter and summer, and taking countermeasures as necessary.

It is sensible to provide natural shade for a pond with big trees, for instance. This effectively prevents the water overheating in summer and thus prevents excessive evaporation. In winter so-called ice inhibitors (see p.111) ensure the all-important gas exchange with the air, so the fish are sure to survive.

Technology in water gardening

MOST THINGS WON'T WORK WITHOUT TECHNOLOGY

Whether you've got a pond or a water course, a spring stone, or a pond in a container, it's difficult to conceive of water gardening without technology. Pumps that transport the water in a closed circuit or ensure water circulation are almost always needed. And aids such as filter systems are usually needed to maintain water quality.

When planning your water technology, it is worth choosing an ecologically sensible option, such as safeguarding energy consumption via renewable energy sources, and water supplies from natural sources. In the process, consider pumps powered by solar power and water supplied from a water butt or a natural spring.

In the case of water course and pond supply, it is possible to minimize energy consumption using the shortest, most efficient recirculation of water. The more water flowing visibly, the more must also be pumped back from the reservoir to the source. In turn the water flow is not determined by the length of the water course alone, but also by the gradient and water course width.

Pumps

A pump is not always a pump—you must choose carefully depending on where you are going to use it and the job it will have to do. Basically, water gardening pumps can be divided into the following three categories:

▬ CIRCULATION PUMP: The pump is placed at the bottom of the pond at the deepest possible point. It circulates the water and thus ensures an adequate oxygen supply. Branded product manufacturers recommend these pumps for use in combination with a filter system as well (see below).

- WATER COURSE PUMP: This type of pump is very powerful and thus able to transport the water from the end of a water course to a distant source.

- SPRING/FOUNTAIN PUMP: This type of pump is specially designed for water features. It is usually sold with an extensible telescopic pipe, which directs the water to the surface of the pond, and a special fountain fitting. Floating pumps, which function on the surface of the water, are an unusual feature. They are especially suitable for muddy ponds where it is difficult to install a pump at the bottom.

CHARACTERISTICS AND OPERATING POINT

Most importantly, pumps must be perfectly matched to the water in terms of performance, the decisive factor being the height to which the water has to be pumped, and the volume.

This is demonstrated by the pump's characteristics, expressed in a system of coordinates for every pump. The units of measurement are, on the one hand, the pump height (H) in feet (or meters) and, on the other, the volume (Q) in gallons (or liters). From these characteristics it is possible to

determine precisely how much water the pump should be able to transport for a specific height.

In order to buy the correct pump you need to know the necessary operating point, i.e. exactly how much water you want to carry to what height.

If you don't have much prior experience you will find it difficult to estimate correctly the volumes of water to be transported, which is why we recommend buying your pump from a specialist dealer, who will be able to provide you with expert advice.

Water purification

There are various technical devices available commercially for purifying water and maintaining water quality. These lighten the load considerably and make water gardening more pleasurable:

■ FILTRATION SYSTEM: Where smaller ponds are concerned, water's self-cleaning ability is often inadequate to restore the balance or maintain it permanently. This is why it is worth giving Nature a helping hand with a filter system. This directs the water through a circulation pump to a filter chamber where various filters are suspended. These collect impurities and clear the water. In addition, devices known as biological filtration systems are available commercially. These biologically degrade additional impurities in the water, such as excess nutrients. The choice of filters is very wide, so expert advice is essential when buying.

■ SKIMMER: Skimmer is the term used to describe purification systems that suction particles of dirt off the water surface. There are various versions of these machines, some more powerful than others, for ponds of differing sizes.

VACUUM: In the course of a year, organic materials, sand, and particles of dirt are deposited on the floor of the pond, creating what is known as sludge. If this is not removed the pond silts up over time. The pond can be cleaned biologically by adding special bacteria cultures (available from specialist shops). To clean a pond manually, it is usually necessary to drain the water, unless you use an appropriate pond vacuum. It works just like a household vacuum cleaner and sucks the impurities up from the pond floor.

OXIDATOR: This system allows the water's oxygen content to be enriched effectively without electric pumps. The oxidator is filled with oxidator solution (hydrogen peroxide) and distilled water. The mixture is sunk into the pond in a special plastic container, where it steadily gives off oxygen into the water. When the solution has been exhausted, the oxidator floats up to the surface of the water and can be filled up again.

ICE INHIBITOR: Fish and aquatic plants need oxygen in winter too. A permanently frozen pond surface prevents the necessary exchange of gases with the air. This is why it is important to keep an oxygen hole in the pond free of ice using a special ice inhibitor. Alternatively, you can, of course, smash a hole in the ice on a regular basis. An oxidator also prevents a pond from freezing over completely.

SOLAR TECHNOLOGY

Smaller pumps and lights in and around the water do not need lots of power; they can be provided with an environmentally friendly supply derived from solar energy. Special solar devices are available from specialist shops; some of these are tailored precisely to a pump's power requirements.

A to Z of plants

Personal taste

Of course it is not only the design of ponds or water courses—whether as functional or visual features—that determines the impact created by gardening with water. The picture is only complete with the plants. They bring the garden alive.

We distinguish between three types of plants. First, there are those that live in water and are extremely important for ecological balance.

Plants with floating leaves, such as water lilies, are of particular interest to water gardeners but, where appearance is concerned, it is mainly the second group, of marginal plants that root in wet ground and cover the banks, that is much more important. They are more eye-catching because of their height. The third category of water gardening plants is all those that do especially well in close proximity to water, as well as trees and shrubs that provide valuable shade along the banks.

There is a range of plants that are commonly associated very closely with water gardening. We introduce the most important over the next few pages, in almost 100 plant portraits.

The selection does not purport to be complete and reflects the editors' preferences. In part the portraits introduce in more detail specific subspecies that are especially suitable for water gardening or that are extremely popular.

INFO BOXES

To make it easier to choose plants for your own garden, we have included a little info box with every plant portrait. The top symbol indicates whether the plant prefers a sunny, semishaded or shaded position.

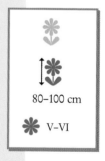

The second line gives the height to which the plant grows, which may vary greatly depending on plant type. In the case of several species the details relate to the commonest types. The body text indicates which varieties may be higher or lower growing.

Finally, the flowering season is given in months, using Roman numerals, next to the flower symbol. If the plant description does not include a flower symbol, then this information is not available.

Acer palmatum

Maple

100–400 cm

V–VI

The botanical name Acer is derived from Latin, and roughly means sharp or pointed, a reference to the maple's characteristic leaf form. Evergreen or deciduous maple trees are found throughout the woods of Europe, North Africa, and Asia, as well as Central and North America.

Acer palmatum, also known as cut-leaf maple, is a variety that is especially suitable for water gardening, because its height of 13 to 20 ft (4 to 6 m) is not too tall. The tree has a wide spread and from May to June bears purplish-red blossoms, which develop into red fruit in late summer. The vibrant green of the leaves in summer is transformed into wonderful, glowing shades of yellow, orange, and red in autumn.

One example of a highly decorative variety is *dissectum atropurpureum*, (dwarf) the Japanese red cut-leaf maple, which grows very slowly and rarely exceeds 5 ft (1.5 m). It is especially striking because of its remarkable, finely cut, red leaves.

Maples prefer a sunny to slightly shaded position, sheltered from the wind, and moist, rich soil. Because they like a high level of humidity, beside a garden pond is the perfect place for them. They are displayed to best advantage as a single, medium-sized specimen.

Achillea

Yarrow or milfoil

The common milfoil (*Achillea millefolium*) has long been known as a medicinal plant that prevents inflammation and cramps, has an antiseptic effect, and assists clotting. Legend has it that it was also used as a medicinal herb by the Greek hero Achilles during the Trojan War, lending the plant its botanical name of *Achillea*.

There are many different varieties of milfoil. Because it naturally occurs in damp meadows or beside water, *Achillea ptarmica*, also known as sneezewort, is ideally suited to water gardening. It has narrow, undivided, serrated leaves. The white flower heads, grouped in loose, flat-topped clusters, or cymes, appear between June and September. The plants grow to 1 to 3 ft (30 to 100 cm) high.

In water gardens the decorative milfoil is suitable for marginal or boggy areas of ponds and water courses. It prefers a sunny to semi-shaded position and moist soil. The flowering period can be extended by dead heading. Popular varieties are the compact "Nana Compacta," just 1 ft (30 cm) high, and the bushy "Snowball," around 2 ft (60 cm) high, whose brilliant white, ball-shaped flower heads are reminiscent of little pompoms, or even snowballs!

30–100 cm

VI–IX

Adiantum pedatum

MAIDENHAIR FERN

15–60 cm

Adiantum pedatum, also called maidenhair fern, is common in woods and beside water in North America and northeast Asia. The botanical designation *Adiantum* (Greek *a* as a negation, *dianein* for "covered with tears") describes the water droplets running off the edges of the fronds; *pedatum* describes the foot-shaped leaf.

The perennial maidenhair fern has pale green fronds that rise from fan-shaped leaves, which sit at the end of long, dark brownish-black, shiny stalks. In autumn the fronds assume a beautiful golden yellow color. The plant grows from 6 to 24 in (15 to 60 cm) tall.

In water gardening this decorative fern is suitable for growing beneath trees or to accompany tall plants along banks. The attractive fronds can create an almost tropical atmosphere along the edges of standing or slow-flowing water.

Adiantum pedatum is particularly at home in semi-shaded to shaded locations. It will grow best on well-drained, moist soil. Although the plant is hardy, we recommend protecting the shoots from late frosts.

Alisma plantago-aquatica

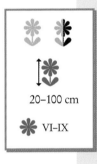

20–100 cm

VI–IX

Water plantain

Alisma plantago-aquatica is a native of water verges, ditches, and ponds, as well as marshy meadows, in Europe, Asia, and Africa.

Together with the rosettes of ovate to lanceolate green leaves, the plant's flower heads are extremely decorative. The numerous little white to pale pink flowers appear between June and September. *Alisma plantago-aquatica* reaches 8 in to 3 ft (20 to 100 cm) high.

A particularly useful characteristic of water plantain is that, like other plants that live in areas of standing water, it can cope with fluctuating water levels. It is very happy in standing water 2 to 12 in (5 to 30 cm) deep, but also flourishes in marshy, wet ground, and can cope with the occasional flood. It prefers full sun or partial shade. In a water garden, water plantain is well suited to boggy areas, or areas of standing or slow-flowing water. A very attractive setting can be achieved when it is combined with flowering rush, water mint, marsh trefoil, or various types of iris.

Anemone japonica

Windflower

Anemone, or windflower, is a genus with around 100 species, primarily found in the northern hemisphere, and mostly in the Asian temperate zones. They became popular ornamental plants in Central European gardens, which they adorn with their splendid blooms at various times of year, depending on species and variety.

The rather fragile-looking flowers have always been symbolic of innocence, trust, transitoriness, and vulnerability. Yet appearances are deceptive, because anemones are in fact rather undemanding and easy-to-care-for plants, and thus a useful addition to water gardening.

30–120 cm

✳ VIII–X

Born of the goddess Flora's jealousy

The name anemone comes from anemos, the Greek word for "wind." Myth has it that Anemona was one of the goddess Flora's nymphs. When her husband, god of the wind Zephyr, fell in love with Anemona, jealous Flora transformed her into a flower, which has born the name anemone, or windflower, ever since, because the delicate flowers move at the slightest breeze.

A very attractive species is *Anemone japonica*, also known as Japanese anemone, or autumn anemone. It prefers partially shaded sites and moist, humus-rich soil, such as is found near to water. It blooms between August and October. It is typified by the long, firm stalks bearing blossoms in late summer that glow brightly from the semi-shade. These plants can grow to 1 to 4 ft (30 to 120 cm). *Anemone japonica* flowers in white, silvery pink, purple red, dark pink, and rose pink, some with semi-double blossoms. Familiar varieties are white "Honorine Jobert," or purplish-red "Prinz Heinrich."

Aruncus

GOAT'S BEARD OR CUTLEAF

Goat's beard is also known by the botanical name *Aruncus sylvester,* or *Aruncus dioicus.* In the wild the plant occurs in damp woodland in northern temperate zones.

130–200 cm

VI–VII

The vigorous plant grows to a height of 4 to 6 ft (130 to 200 cm). Its large, green leaves are divided into bipinnate leaflets with serrated edges. In the flowering season it bears small white to yellowish-white flowers that stand in widely spaced, branching panicles up to 20 in (50 cm) long. The heads are still extremely decorative even when they have finished flowering and can be used, for example, in floral arrangements.

Goat's beard is one of the few plants that manages with little sun. It is relatively undemanding, but prefers damp, rich soil. This attractive plant is valued by water gardeners for brightening up sites that are partially shaded to shaded. Its striking foliage makes *Arunculus sylvester* a suitable ornamental plant for the water's edge. The plant looks very good as a single specimen. A popular variety is "Kneiffi," with very delicately cut, fern-like leaves and creamy white flowers.

Asplenium trichomanes

MAIDENHAIR SPLEENWORT

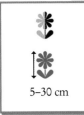

5–30 cm

Asplenium trichomanes, also known as maidenhair spleenwort, or common maidenhair, occurs throughout the world as a wide range of different species. In the wild it is commonly found on damp, shaded rocks, slopes, or tree stumps.

At a height of just 2 to 12 in (5 to 30 cm), the maidenhair spleenwort is especially suitable for small gardens. It has unipinnate, matte green, perennial fronds and shiny, brownish-black stems. The leaves are single-stemmed, elliptical, or elongated and have rounded tips.

A fern's attractive appearance ensures a tropical atmosphere in your garden.

They are very well suited to shady banks, for example, where they are not only decorative, but also enjoy optimum growing conditions. Like most ferns, the maidenhair spleenwort prefers partial to full shade. As far as soil is concerned it is not choosy, but grows especially well in chalky, loamy, and humus-rich soil. Familiar varieties include "Ramo Cristatum" or "Incisum."

Astilbe

Pink and red astilbes have been bred from the original white-flowering species by cross-breeding, sowing, and selecting. Together with *astilbe chinensis-pumila* hybrids, *Astilbe japonica* hybrids and *Astilbe simplicifolia* hybrids, *Astilbe arendsii* hybrids are particularly decorative and also very suitable for water gardening.

Astilbes are characterized by medium height, luxuriant growth, and delicate pinnate leaves. The colors range from pure white, to delicate pink, to dark red.

The plants look very attractive when planted in bright to semi-shaded positions at the water's edge. If they are in direct sunlight they need thorough watering. Hybrids of *arendsii* are somewhat more demanding in terms of soil and light than the other kinds, but there is considerable variation between the different types, of which the following are well known and extremely popular:

■ "BRIDE'S VEIL": This variety develops loose, overhanging, veil-like panicles of white flowers that give the plant its name. It grows to 2 to 3 ft (60 to 80 cm) and flowers between July and September.

■ "FANAL": An eye-catching variety with striking, pomegranate-pink flowers that appear between July and September on plants 2 to 2 ft 6 in (60 to 70 cm) tall.

■ "FIRE": This astilbe variety also bears its ruby red panicles between July and September and achieves heights of around 3 ft (80 cm).

60–80 cm

VII–IX

Astrantia

MASTERWORT

30–80 cm

V–IX

Masterwort's distribution in Europe stretches from Spain, across the Balkans, to the Caucasus. In the Alps it is still encountered frequently at altitudes exceeding 6,000 ft (2,000 m).

This wild plant's particular beauty lies in its unusual star-shaped flowers. The many tiny individual flowers are actually unprepossessing, but are surrounded by a wreath of pinkish-white, pointed bracts and an elegant star-shaped collar. Occasionally gardeners look for plants that grow and bloom in shadier places. This is one of them. In water gardens the master-wort flourishes in a site that receives little sun, provided the ground is wet enough. A differentiation should be made between the greater and lesser masterwort. *Astrantia major* grows 2 to 3 ft (50 to 80 cm) high, while *Astrantia minor,* better suited to smaller plots, only grows to about 1 ft (30 cm). There are various species in numerous shades of pink, white, and deep red. "Rosea," for example, is a 2 ft (70 cm) plus hybrid with red-dish flowers which is also suitable for wetter sites. "Primadonna" is also a red-flowered variety.

Bergenia purpurascens

BERGENIA

20–60 cm

✳ III–V

Evergreen bergenias, with their large, round leathery broadleaves, are a noteworthy addition to any garden throughout the year. They are also relatively easy to care for and are not very demanding in terms of soil. These properties make them very popular ornamental plants for water gardeners too.

The vigorous plants have strong, creeping roots. In spring, between March and May, fat, flat-topped clusters of flowers, composed of many bell-shaped individual flowers, push upwards on the fleshy stalks. Depending on the species and variety, these glow in red, pink, or white. Other varieties also bloom later in the year. A very impressive species is *Bergenia purpurascens*. Its decorative, deep green leaves are purplish-red on the underside. In winter the whole leaf turns red. The flowers, also purplish-red, appear between April and May. The plant grows to around 1 ft 6 in (45 cm).

Bergenias prefer a sunny to partially shaded site. They flourish in rich, damp, well-drained soil, but also tolerate more inhospitable conditions. These robust plants with their decorative leaves and beautiful flowers are suitable for shaping the edges of a water garden's streams or banks.

Blechnum

Hard fern

Blechnum, also known by the name hard fern, is a genus of 150 to 200 mostly evergreen species of fern, mainly encountered in damp and sheltered sites in the wild.

In water gardens the decidedly decorative hard fern is a valuable addition in designing semi-shaded to shaded areas. Species of *Blechnum* brighten up the water's edge with their attractive fronds and fresh green shades. If several specimens are grouped together, they create a pleasing picture. The hard fern prefers moist to damp and acidic soils. We briefly introduce two well-known subspecies here:

10–50 cm

■ BLECHNUM PENNA MARINA: This subspecies is also known by the botanical name *Blechnum alpinum*, or the common name alpine water fern. It is distributed throughout Australia and South America. Externally it is similar to *Blechnum spicant*, but is more delicate. The sterile fronds carry elongated to triangular leaves, while the fertile fronds' plumes are narrow and elongated. The plant reaches 4 to 8 in (10 to 20 cm) in height.

■ BLECHNUM SPICANT: This species, found throughout Europe, northern Asia, and North America, is also known as common deer fern. The evergreen plants are especially characterized by their elegant, upright growth and the delicate fronds. The sterile fronds are around 8 to 16 in (20 to 40 cm) tall and unipinnate. They are shiny dark green and look leathery. The young plants form regular rosettes that lie flat. Older plants develop fertile fronds that can be up to 2 ft 6 in (70 cm) tall. *Blechnum spicant* grows to around 8 to 20 in (20 to 50 cm) in height.

Butomus umbellatus

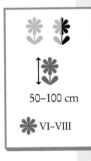

50–100 cm

❋ VI–VIII

Flowering rush

Butomus umbellatus, common in all the temperate zones of Europe and Asia, is also known as flowering rush. It is characterized by its very decorative flower heads and is indeed one of the loveliest bog plants. These attractive plants are very popular for ornamental use in water gardens.

The perennial flowering rush bears basal, elongated, three-sided dark green leaves, over which the umbelliferous, long-stemmed flower heads are suspended between June and August. These especially ornamental blooms are generally pink with dark red veining, but there are also white varieties. Well-known varieties include deep pink "Rose Red" or white "Snow White." The flowering rush grows to around 16 in to 3 ft (50 to 100 cm) in height.

The plants prefer a wet location in sun to partial shade, and are able to grow in 8 to 16 in (20 to 50 cm) of water. The soil should be muddy and nutrient rich. Water gardeners grow the flowering rush, with its beautiful blooms, along banks next to standing or slow-flowing water.

Calla palustris

Bog arum or water arum or wild calla

Calla palustris, a native of bogs and banks alongside standing or flowing water in northern, central, and eastern Europe, as well as northern Asia and North America, is also known as bog arum.

The characteristic feature of this plant is its flower. A greenish to yellowish spadex is surrounded by a white spathe similar in shape to a leaf. The bog arum flowers between May and August. The shiny, bright green to dark green leaves are heart shaped. Bog arum grows 6 to 12 in (15 to 30 cm) high.

Calla palustris is not particularly fussy about light and does equally well in sunny positions or shade, but the roots should not be allowed to dry out. A constant water depth of 2 to 4 in (5 to 10 cm) is perfect for optimum growth. Care should be taken when handling this plant, because all parts of it are extremely poisonous and can cause skin irritation. In water gardening the decorative bog arum is good for the banks of standing or slow-flowing water, grouped with marsh trefoil, marsh marigold, or rushes.

15–30 cm

V–VIII

Callitriche palustris

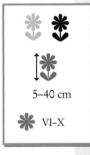

5–40 cm

VI–X

Water starwort

Water starwort is native to the temperate zones of the northern hemisphere, Australia, and New Guinea. In the wild it is mainly found in standing or slow-flowing water.

This evergreen, ornamental, underwater plant anchors itself deep in the pond or stream bed with its roots. It reaches heights of between 2 and 16 in (5 and 40 cm), but the majority of the plant lies under water. The thin, branching shoots rise to the surface of the water, where they form decorative, star-shaped rosettes of little, spade-shaped leaves. The unprepossessing flowers that appear at the junctions of the underwater leaves between June and October are usually overlooked.

The relatively undemanding and adaptable water starwort prefers a sunny position, but will grown in semi-shade or shade. The ideal water depth is 12 to 24 in (30 to 60 cm). In ponds or slow-flowing water, this plant is not only a decorative accompaniment to other plants with floating leaves, such as water lily or yellow floating heart, it also produces oxygen, which is essential for the survival of aquatic animals, and important to the water quality.

Caltha palustris

KING CUP OR MARSH MARIGOLD

The king cup is one of the best-known domestic bog plants. It is a native of Europe, Asia, and North America, where it is found in boggy meadows and ditches.

It grows to 6 to 20 in (15 to 50 cm) in height and bears kidney-shaped, jagged, dark green leaves. It brightens up the months between March and May with its glowing, mainly golden-yellow, cup-shaped flowers. This makes it a very popular plant for the edges of ponds and streams in water gardens, because most other plants suitable for the banks do not flower so early. The decorative flowers ensure interest and color, and combine well with golden saxifrage, water avens, or true water forget-me-not.

Caltha palustris does best in nutrient-rich, boggy areas. It prefers full sun to partial shade. If it is standing in water, the depth should be no more than 4 in (10 cm). Well-known varieties of king cup include white flowering "Alba," which reaches heights of 15 to 20 centimeters (6 to 8 inches), or golden-yellow, bushy, 30 centimeters (12 inches) high "*Multiplex.*"

15–50 cm

III–V

Canna indica

Indian shot

Canna indica, also known by the name Indian shot, is a decorative sight in a water garden because of its big, exotic-looking blooms. The plant is a native of tropical and subtropical America.

The vigorous, upright plant bears large, ovate to elongated, dark green leaves. The bunches or panicles of lily-like flowers appear from June to October.

There are a number of different hybrids in brilliant red, soft orange, and shades of yellow, with the flowers having single or multiple patterns. Depending on the variety, the plant can reach a height of 1 to 6 ft (30 to 220 cm).

The attractive column of flowers, with its strikingly bright blooms, ensures a colorful and exotic accent at the water's edge. It grows best in a sunny, sheltered site and in nutrient-rich, damp soil. The plant requires a good water supply and always needs to be well-watered. It will flower almost permanently if the dead blooms are removed. Because *Canna indica* is very sensitive to frost, it should be overwintered at temperatures above 50°F (10°C).

30–220 cm

VI–X

Carex grayi

SEDGE GLOBE

Carex, also called sedge, grows naturally in swamps, on moors, in wet woodland, or by water. The plant looks especially attractive because of its patterned or colorful foliage. Some species' flowers or fruits are also highly decorative.

An appealing species, originally native to North America, is *Carex grayi*, also known by the name sedge globe. Its characteristic decorative fruit gave rise to this name.

This thick, bushy plant has erect spikes of bright green leaves. The relatively unprepossessing mid-green flower spikes, which later develop into the interesting pale green fruit heads, appear between June and August. The plant may reach heights of 16 to 30 in (40 to 80 cm).

Carex grayi is ideally suited for use along the banks of your garden pond because of its architectural shape. It prefers a position in full sun to partial shade and likes rich, damp to wet soil. The fruits look very good as a decorative addition to dried flower arrangements.

40–80 cm

VI–VIII

Caryopteris

40–100 cm

VII–IX

BLUEBEARD

The small shrub *Caryopteris*, also known by the name bluebeard, originally came from Mongolia and northern China.

Bluebeard's blue to violet flowers appear from July to September and form an interesting contrast to the elongated, grey-green leaves.

The plant grows into a wide bush around 2 ft 6 in to 3 ft (80 to 100 cm) high. A particular feature of bluebeard is the lemony, spicy, aromatic scent of the leaves.

In the water garden bluebeard is a decidedly attractive, late summer bloomer, with its beautiful blue flowers. It prefers a sunny site sheltered from the wind and light, well-drained soil. In cold winters the shoots die back with frost, but if cut back they will shoot again in early spring.

One of the most popular and most attractive varieties is "Heavenly Blue." It has particularly striking violet flowers and grows 2 to 3 ft (60 to 100 cm) high.

Cedrus atlantica

Atlas cedar

1–30 m

IX–X

All species of cedar are popular, primarily for their decorative, usually unconventional growth and grey-green needles, and are shown to best advantage as single specimens. Because these evergreen trees can grow 3 to 12 ft (1 to 4 m), they are best suited to large gardens.

The atlas cedar is originally a native of the Atlas Mountains in Algeria and Morocco. Initially it is wide and conical in shape but over time the crown loosens up increasingly. The branches bristle with squiggly, blue-green clumps of needles. *Cedrus atlantica* does best in a sunny, sheltered site. The soil should be moderately dry to moist and be well drained.

An extremely decorative and well-known variety is "Glauca Pendula." It is striking not only because of its silver-grey needles but also its mane-like, hanging shoots. The branches are almost horizontal and the tips point downwards. At 12 to 18 ft (4 to 6 m) it is not as tall and imposing as other species of cedar, so it is ideally suited to smaller gardens. The striking, weeping shape can make it a very attractive addition to a water garden.

Ceratophyllum demersum

Coontail or hornwarts

Ceratophyllum demersum, also called coontail, is encountered is standing and slow-flowing water in the wild.

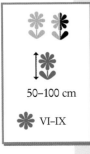

50–100 cm

VI–IX

This free-floating underwater plant forms shoots that may be 20 to 36 in (50 to 100 cm). Although it is rootless, *Ceratophyllum demersum* is able to anchor itself in muddy ground using its colorless shoots. The rough, dark green leaves are set with tiny, pointed thorns. Small, white or green, unprepossessing flowers develop between June and September.

Because coontail often grows under water and also looks extremely ordinary, it is not really used for decorative purposes in water gardening. It does offer the water gardener some other advantages, though. Because it grows rapidly the plant consumes nutrients well and it filters excess nutrients out of the pond. As a result the water remains clear and algae do not form. Furthermore, coontail is a superb oxygenator and thus ensures a healthy balance in the pond. The shifting carpet it forms offers fish protection from enemies, such as cats.

Despite these positive attributes, take care that this plant, which tends towards mass growth, does not overgrow small

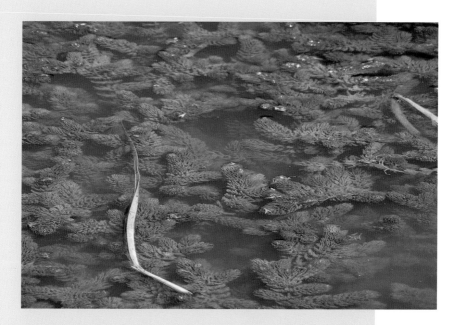

ponds too quickly, or smother other aquatic plants. If the plant becomes too thick it should be cleared occasionally to restrict growth. Coontail dies back in autumn—its tough thorns then sink back to the floor of the pond or stream, to form new plants in spring.

Ceratophyllum demersum grows best in the sun, but also tolerates partial shade. The water should be rich in nutrients and can be up to 5 ft (150 cm) deep.

Cimicifuga

Bugbane

Cimicifuga, also commonly known by the name bugbane, is characterized by its decorative, impressive blooms. It is native to northern temperate areas, where it is mostly found in damp, shady, grassy or wooded sites.

The plant's green or brownish broadleaf foliage is pinnate and has a heavily serrated edge. Depending on the species and variety, the lovely, white or cream panicles appear on long, thin stalks between July and October. Bugbane can grow to be 16 in to 6 ft (40 to 200 cm) tall.

Cimicifuga prefers a place in partial or full shade that is as protected from the wind as possible. It grows best in moist to damp, humus-rich soil. Its attractive flower candles provide nice splashes of color.

Popular species

- *CIMICIFUGA RACE-MOSA:* This species is also called snakeroot. The flowers appear between July and August and it grows up to 6 ft (200 cm) tall.

- *CIMICIFUGA RAMOSA:* Branched bugbane bears its flowers between September and October. One of the best-known varieties is "Atropurpurea," which bears reddish-brown foliage.

- *CIMICIFUGA SIMPLEX:* This species, also known as snakeroot, or black cohosh, flowers from September to October.

Overall this plant reaches 16 in to 4 ft (40 to 130 cm) in height. Well-known varieties are "Armleuchter" with strongly branching candles of flowers, "Braunlaub" with dark brownish-green leaves, and "White Pearl" with little branching, and very pale green foliage.

40–200 cm

VII–X

Cornus kousa

KOUSA DOGWOOD OR JAPANESE DOGWOOD

Cornus kousa, the kousa dogwood, is a native of the summer woods of Japan and Korea. This large, elegant shrub may reach a height of 15 to 21 ft (5 to 7 m), initially assuming a vase shape, then spreading outward.

The ovate to elliptical, pointed tipped leaves are dark green on top and bluish underneath. Later in the year they turn brilliant yellow or scarlet red, making this attractive plant easy on the eye in autumn. The little greenish-yellow flower heads, which appear from May to June, are encased by white, elongated ovoid secondary bracts like the petals of a flower. They mature into little, spherical, pink to reddish fruit.

Both flowers and foliage make *Cornus kousa* a popular ornamental plant in water gardens, where it is especially decorative at the water's edge. The plant prefers a sunny to partially shaded site and enjoys humus-rich, well-drained soil. Examples of well-known varieties include "Gold Star" with white and yellow-patterned leaves, or "Milky Way" with creamy white secondary bracts and plentiful fruits.

500–700 cm

V–VI

Cotinus coggygria

Smoke bush

The most striking feature of *Cotinus coggygria* is its long, feathery bunches of fruit with reddish colored "hairs," which make the shrub look fuzzy.

This bushy plant can reach a considerable height, 6 to 15 ft (2 to 5 m). It has green, oval leaves that turn a decorative yellow to orange in autumn. The rather unprepossessing, tiny, yellowish-green flowers appear between June and July. The plant is truly eye-catching, though, when it develops its reddish, fuzzy fruits from July.

In a water garden the decorative smoke bush flourishes in a warm, sheltered place in the sun, preferring a chalky, dry to moist soil. It looks best as a single specimen. One exceptional variety is "Royal Purple." It is also called red smoke bush because of the dark purple-red leaves that turn scarlet in autumn. It forms a nice contrast to trees and shrubs with green and yellow foliage.

200–500 cm

VI–VII

Crocosmia "Lucifer"

Montbretia

50–120 cm

VII–IX

Montbretias are a branch of the *Iridaceae*, or Iris family, which consists of just seven bulbed plants originally native to South Africa.

These plants have dense, long, sword-shaped leaves, which may exhibit striking veins or lengthwise creases. A characteristic feature is the curved, overhanging, projecting flowers. They appear between July and September and consist of funnel-shaped individual flowers, arranged in a double-rowed spike. The range of colors extends from yellow, orange, to fiery orange-red. Depending on the variety, the plants may grow 20 in to 4 ft (50 to 120 cm) high.

Montbretia are extremely popular plants because of their long flowering period and attractive blooms, which often adorn the water's edge. They are also very suitable as cut flowers. They will grow best in a warm, sunny to semi-shaded location, with damp, well-drained soil.

One extremely decorative variety is "Lucifer," which is very striking because of its fiery tomato and orange-red flowers that open upwards with wide, slightly curving heads. This plant attains heights of 3 to 4 ft (90 to 120 cm).

Cyperus alternifolius

Umbrella plant or Nile grass

Cyperus alternifolius, with its slightly exotic appearance, is a decorative plant originally from Madagascar.

What is special about this compact, bushy plant is the umbrella-like crown of alternating, elongated, dark green leaves. These radiate out from the ends of the upright stalks. From July to August greenish flower heads emerge from the center of the leafy crown. This grass attains a height of 16 in to 4 ft (50 to 120 cm).

The umbrella plant prefers a site in full sun or partial shade and needs damp, muddy to boggy, nutrient-rich soils. It is suitable for water up to 12 in (30 cm) deep. Because this warmth-loving plant is not hardy, it should be overwintered indoors and not returned to the pond before the end of May. We therefore recommend that it be planted in a container. This interesting grass does well in marginal areas of standing or slow-flowing water. Single specimens look especially good.

50–120 cm

VII–VIII

Eichhornia crassipes

WATER HYACINTH

15–20 cm

VI–IX

The water hyacinth is an exotic floating plant native to tropical and subtropical America, where it occurs in lakes, ponds, or very slow-flowing water.

Eichhornia crassipes is carried above water by its spherical, swollen, air-filled leaf stalks. With thick bunches of roots that hang deep into the water, the plant can absorb nutrients directly from it.

The unusual, rounded, shiny pale green leaves are arranged in rosettes and are a valuable addition to any garden pond. The water hyacinth is even more attractive between July and September, when the luxuriant, pale purple flowers appear, standing in hyacinth-like spears. The plants generally achieve a height of 6 to 8 in (15 to 20 cm).

Eichhornia crassipes's unusual foliage and flowers conjure an exotic, tropical atmosphere in a water garden. It is worth bearing in mind, though, that because of its origins the plant needs a lot of warmth, and is not hardy everywhere. Accordingly, the water hyacinth prefers a site in full sun and water that is as warm as possible. It should be overwintered in a bright, warm room.

Elodea canadensis

Canadian pondweed

Elodea canadensis – Canadian pondweed – originally came from the temperate latitudes of North America and spread to Europe in the mid-19th century, apparently via Ireland.

The shoots of this underwater plant can reach lengths of 8 in to 3 ft (20 to 100 cm). Its curly leaves are tightly packed along the shoots. They are small, dark green, and lance-shaped. The plant does not bloom very often; when it does, the rather unassuming flowers appear between May and August.

Canadian pondweed spreads very rapidly and can smother other aquatic plants. This should be prevented by timely and regular thinning out. It is not exactly suitable for enhancing a pond, but is an important oxygenator, and its cleaning action contributes to establishing and maintaining healthy water conditions.

20–100 cm

V–VIII

A WAILING AND A GNASHING OF TEETH

As early as the start of the last century, the unchecked spread of Canadian pondweed was a hot topic, even in the media. According to a German newspaper of October 9th, 1910, "Everywhere there arose a wailing and a gnashing of teeth, because it seemed that the day was not far off when all the inland waters of Europe would be stuffed to the brim with this weed, that no ship could sail, no one could bathe, no duck could dabble, and no fish swim."

Eriophorum

COTTON GRASS

A particular feature of *Eriophorum* is the decorative, dense, white fruit heads that look like little cotton balls, leading to the common name cotton grass. This plant occurs naturally on boggy land and moors.

Cotton grass reaches 6 to 20 in (15 to 50 cm) in height and, depending on the growing conditions, may be perennial. It has grass-like, narrow, linear leaves. The silvery-grey to brown flower heads appear between April and May. Between June and July, the seed heads described above develop, and these are what make the grass such a popular decorative plant.

Eriophorum is a typical moorland plant and therefore can only tolerate lime-free, acidic soil with few nutrients. It loves full sun. When planting it, bear in mind that cotton grass is not very competitive and is quickly smothered by other plants. We recommend planting it around 18 in (50 cm) away from neighboring plants. In a water garden it is best suited to marginal planting beside moorland ponds, in moorland beds, or on the banks of a pond, where it will tolerate water up to 2 in (5 cm) deep.

15–50 cm

IV–V

Popular species

- *ERIOPHORUM ANGUSTIFOLIUM:* Also known as narrowleaved cotton grass, this species puts out runners and grows relatively quickly. There are three to five spikes at the end of the upright stalks.

- *ERIOPHORUM LATIFOLIUM:* This species is also known as broadleaved cotton grass, which means that this plant's foliage is rather broader than in the case of narrowleaved cotton grass. It does not put out runners. Both species have flower heads that are similar.

Eupatorium

JOE PYE WEED OR MIST-FLOWER

50–180 cm

VII–IX

The long-flowering Joe Pye weed's decorative, abundant flower heads are especially ornamental for water gardens. The plants are naturally sited in woodlands, in clearings, and on damp paths and banks.

This impressive plant, 18 in to 6 ft (50 to 180 cm) tall, carries palmate, broadleaf pinnate foliage that is green to dark green. The beautiful little flower heads, which are pink, copper-orange, purple, or white, depending on the variety, appear between July and September. The panicles of flowers don't just attract people, they also entice bees and butterflies. Popular varieties are purplish-pink "Plenum" or white "Alba."

Planted in groups in a water garden, Joe Pye weed is almost perfect for landscaping the banks of standing or flowing water. This plant prefers chalky, humus-containing, moist to damp soil, and does well in a sunny to semi-shaded place. Although it is relatively robust, in very hot summers make sure that it gets enough water. The dried flower heads are very pretty in autumn.

Filipendula

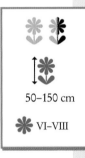

50–150 cm

VI–VIII

Meadowsweet

In the past *Filipendula ulmaria*, also known as meadowsweet, was often used as a medicine to counteract fever and pain. In the wild this plant grows in damp places, such as along banks, in ditches, or on water-logged meadows.

Meadowsweet's striking, tall flower heads are a spectacular sight in a water garden. The stems rise from pinnate, dark green, broad leaves, with fine white hairs on the undersides. The countless tiny white flowers form a many-branched, flat-topped cluster of flowers. They appear between June and August, and emit a powerful, honey-like scent. *Filipendula ulmaria* achieves an impressive height from around 18 in to 5 ft (50 to 150 cm).

This plant likes full sun or partial shade. The soil should be damp to wet, and rich in nutrients. In a water garden, meadowsweet is wonderfully suited to the transitional area between the bank and bog zone of standing or flowing water.

It is very attractive when planted with purple loosestrife, golden globes, or late-blooming species of iris.

Gaura

Whirling butterflies or butterfly gaura

Gaura, also called whirling butterflies, is a genus of annual, biennial, hardy perennial and half-hardy perennial species, originally native to North America. It is mostly found in rather damp locations in the wild.

The plant has alternating leaves, which can be lanceolate, elliptical, or spade shaped. The pink to white flowers that bloom from July to October are mostly grouped loosely in fours. Depending on the species, *Gaura* can achieve heights of 16 to 40 in (40 to 100 cm).

Whirling butterflies may prefer a sheltered, warm site in full sun, but will tolerate partial shade. The soil should be rich and well drained. This decorative plant is especially popular because of its exceptionally long flowering period. In water gardens its attractive and striking appearance ensures a scenic picture. The two best-known species are *Gaura biennes,* and *Gaura lindheimerei.* "Siskiyou Pink," with its compact habit and dark foliage, and especially its charming, bright pink and red flowers, is a wonderful eye-catching variety of the latter species.

40–100 cm

VII–X

Hemerocallis

DAY LILY

Hemerocallis acquired its common name because the individual flowers only live for a day. New buds form all the time, though, so the attractive blooms ensure bursts of color in a water garden from May to September.

There is a vast wealth of varieties of this splendid flowering plant. It bears grass- or lily-like leaves, the blossoms may be spider- or star-shaped, triangular, round, or double. The color palette extends from yellow and apricot, to red, brown, or mauve.

Depending on the variety, day lilies may grow to be 1 to 4 ft (30 to 120 cm). These strong plants grow well in sunny to semi-shaded positions, and in rich, damp, well-drained soil. The splendid flowers are especially eye-catching along the banks of garden ponds or water courses. Here are just a few examples of the incredible range of hybrids: "American Revolution": dark purple-brown to deep red flowers; "Corky": lemon yellow flowers; "Green Flutter": pale yellow flowers shading to green; "Prairie Blue Eyes": mauve-blue to lavender-blue; "Sammy Russel": red; "Stella de Oro": brilliant yellow flowers.

30–120 cm

V–IX

Hippuris vulgaris

Mare's tail

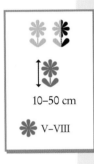

10–50 cm

V–VIII

Hippuris vulgaris forms interesting and highly decorative fronds that look like tiny fir trees. It is mainly found in standing or slow-flowing water.

The plant's upright stalks carry spiraling, lanceolate, needle-like, dark green leaves. The little greenish flowers that bloom from May to August are really unobtrusive. *Hippuris vulgaris* can be 4 to 20 in (10 to 50 cm) tall, with only 6 to 8 in (15 to 20 cm) standing above water.

In deeper water, mare's tail is purely an underwater plant. It is much more decorative in shallower areas near banks, when the shoots spread out over the water and create a miniature pine forest on the water's surface with their attractive fronds. This easy-to-care-for and highly adaptable plant can make its home in either sun or shade, where it prefers limy water. It can be prevented from spreading too luxuriantly by planting it in containers. Mare's tail is also valued by water gardeners for its water purifying properties.

Hosta

FUNKIA OR PLANTAIN LILY

The funkia, also called the plantain lily, is not only prized for its attractive flowers that bloom white, blue and violet between June and September. The heart-shaped to lanceolate leaves are highly decorative too, and offer a rich variety of shapes and colors. It has been used as a garden plant in Japan for centuries. Nowadays a wealth of different species and varieties are available, attaining heights of 8 to 36 in (20 to 90 cm).

The long-lived plant clusters are superbly suited to sites in partial or full shade. They prefer moist to damp, humus-rich soil.

The colorful leaves of some varieties offer varied planting options in water gardens. The decorative foliage looks especially pleasing beside the water's edge and forms an interesting contrast to the colorful flowers. Examples of suitable accompanying plants are monkshood, mountain geranium, or astilbes, as well as various grasses and ferns.

Popular species

20–90 cm

VI–IX

- *HOSTA CRISPULA:* As the common name giant white-edged funkia suggests, this species is particularly noted for its heart-shaped, white-edged leaves that reach sizes of up to 16 in (40 cm). It has lavender-blue to lilac-colored flowers.

- *HOSTA FORTUNEI:* There are many different varieties of what is known as the grey-leaved funkia, which bears white or violet flowers. Well-known examples include "Aurea," with leaves that start out golden yellow, turning pale yellow to green, "Aureo-Marginata" with dark green, yellow-veined leaves, or "Hyacinthina" with grey-blue to grey-green leaves.

- *HOSTA LANCIFOLIA:* So named because of its narrow, lanceolate, dark green leaves. It bears violet flowers.

- *HOSTA SIEBOLDII:* This species has green leaves with white edges. Its flowers are violet or white.

- *HOSTA VENTRICOSA:* Also known as bell funkia. There are green or colored leaved varieties, which all have violet flowers. Well-known species include "Aureomaculata" with dark green, yellow-flecked leaves and "Aureomarginata" with green leaves, edged in cream.

Hydrangea aspera "Macrophylla"

HYDRANGEA

Together with the well-known mophead hydrangeas and climbing hydrangea (*Hydrangea petiolaris*), lacecaps are particularly attractive because of their large, attractive flower heads. This upright, deciduous shrub carries loosely arranged, basal branches and grey-haired shoots. The narrow ovate to lanceolate leaves are dark green on top and covered with filmy hairs underneath.

Hydrangeas can grow into luxuriant bushes exceeding 7 ft (2 m) in height.

150–200 cm

❋ VII–VIII

An especially attractive and frequently cultivated variety is *Hydrangea aspera* "Macrophylla." This fewer branching shrub grows to 5 to 7 ft (150 to 200 cm) and has thick, reddish-brown basal branches. Between July and August the 6 to 12 in (15 to 30 cm) wide, slightly domed, bicolored flower heads appear. The small inner flowers are pinkish-lilac to pale violet, while the outer flowers are white, with slightly serrated edges.

Hydrangeas love semi-shaded sites sheltered from wind and prefer nutrient-rich, moist, humus-heavy soil. They need a lot of water in summer and should be watered thoroughly in extended dry periods. This decorative plant can provide contrasting, extravagant shapes in a water garden. Plants that combine very nicely with *Hydrangea aspera* to create a harmonious picture include ferns, rhododendrons, and types of bamboo.

Hydrocharis morsus-ranae

Frogbit

15–30 cm

VI–VIII

Hydrocharis morsus-ranae is called frogbit because the shape of the green leaves is reminiscent of a frog's mouth. This perennial, runner-forming, floating plant occurs naturally in ditches, ponds, or pools.

The round, heart-shaped, incised, very shiny floating leaves occur in pale green to olive green, occasionally bronze too, and look like little water lily leaves. During the summer the plant forms surface rosettes of leaves, so that a thick carpet may develop very quickly on the water's surface. Very pretty white flowers appear between June and August. In autumn the plants die back, and the buds that have formed previously fall to the floor of the pond. In spring they rise to the surface again, and develop into new plants.

Frogbit is highly recommended for a garden pond, but because it grows very quickly growth should be kept under control by timely thinning out, especially in the case of smaller ponds. In larger ponds, however, luxuriant sprawls can appear very decorative. *Hydrocharis morsus-ranae* prefers a place in shallow water that is almost lime free, and warms up quickly. It may root in water up to 12 in (30 cm) deep or shallow areas close to

banks; otherwise it is free-floating and thus suits any depth of water. The floor of the pond should be muddy to allow the winter buds to survive. The flowers open completely in full sun, but the plant will also tolerate shadier positions.

Because of its pretty floating leaves and attractive flowers, frogbit is a popular decorative plant for water gardening. It looks especially effective in sheltered ponds or along the banks of slow-flowing streams.

Inula

Inula or elecampane

Around 100 different species belong to the genus Inula, which is native to Europe, and the temperate and subtropical areas of Africa and Asia.

Its lovely bright yellow blooms are a very popular addition to water gardens, where it prefers a sunny site, and grows best in moist, well-drained, and rich soil.

Popular species

- *INULA ENSIFOLIA:* Also known as swordleaf inula. The dense bushy plant bears linear to lanceolate, or lanceolate green leaves without stalks, but with fine haired edges. It produces numerous, golden-yellow flower heads between July and September. *Inula ensifolia* grows between 10 to 24 in (25 to 60 cm) high. A very popular variety, especially for smaller water gardens, is "Compacta." It has deep, golden-yellow flower heads and only reaches 6 to 12 in (15 to 30 cm) in height.

15–200 cm

VII–IX

IINULA HELENIUM: This hardy plant is also known as elecampane. It has strong, downy shoots and ovoid or elliptical, serrated leaves that are green, thickly haired on the underside, and have a wavy edge. The brilliant yellow flower heads appear between July and September. This species may attain heights 3 to 6 ft (90 to 180 cm). A component substance in the roots of elecampane has an expectorant effect when used to treat coughs and bronchitis.

Iris

IRIS

The iris is one of the most beautiful garden water garden plants, and its splendid, slightly exotic flowers are an extremely decorative sight appearing along the banks.

The section following is restricted to three species of iris, which have proved their worth in water gardening: *Iris kaempferi*, *Iris laevigata*, and *Iris pseudacorus*. All three prefer damp or wet sites, and full sun or partial shade. They will tolerate water up to 8 in (20 centimeters) deep, making them very suitable for bog gardens, and the damp water's edge, where they are a wonderful sight in full bloom.

POPULAR SPECIES:

- *IRIS KAEMPFERI:* This species is also known by the botanical name *Iris ensata*, commonly called the Japanese iris. It bears bright green leaves on slender stalks. The splendid flowers appear between June and July. They are mostly violet to pale blue, but the wealth of different varieties also includes plants with white or pink flowers. These plants can attain heights of 3 to 4 ft 6 in (60 to 100 cm). During winter this species should not stand directly in water, which is why we recommend container planting.

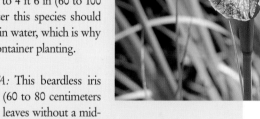

- *IRIS LAEVIGATA:* This beardless iris grows to 2 ft 6 in (60 to 80 centimeters tall. It has smooth leaves without a midrib. The blue to violet flowers, occasionally white or pink in certain varieties, bloom between July and August.

- *IRIS PSEUDACORUS:* This species, which grows between 20 to 40 in (50 to 100 cm) in height, is also called yellow flag iris. It has grass-green, linear, sword-shaped leaves, and pale yellow flowers, which are white in some varieties. This popular species' flowers delight water gardeners from May to June.

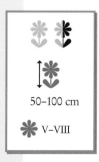

50–100 cm

V–VIII

Juncus maritimus

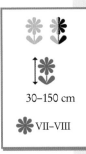

30–150 cm

✳ VII–VIII

Sea rush

The botanical name *Juncus* is derived from the Latin word *jungere*, meaning to "link", or "join," and presumably the plant got its name because in the past, rushes were used for weaving or as a binding. There are around 300 different species of rush worldwide. One that is well suited to water gardens is *Juncus maritimus*, the sea rush. As the name suggests, this salt-tolerating plant is mainly found on sea coasts.

Juncus maritimus can grow to 5 ft (30 to 150 cm). It has linear, dark green leaves, and the rather ordinary flowers are arranged in loose sprays on 4 to 6 in (10 to 15 cm) long flower heads. This plant prefers damp or wet, low nutrient, acidic soil and enjoys full sun or partial shade.

In the water garden sea rush is well suited to damp or wet sites, such as the banks of pools, ditches, or ponds. It contrasts nicely with flowering plants; for a less striking, more integrated picture, combine it with other grasses.

Lemna trisulca

1 cm

VI–VII

STAR DUCKWEED OR IVY-LEAVED DUCKWEED

The greenish flowers of *Lemna trisulca*, also known as ivy duck-weed, or star duckweed, which appear from June to July, are so inconspicuous that they can hardly be distinguished from the surrounding foliage. This floating plant grows to only a half inch (1 centimeter) high; it is fully submerged and floats in loose clumps just below the water's surface.

The undemanding, very easy-to-maintain duckweed prefers standing water, where it will do well irrespective of depth of water and nutrient content. Most species of duckweed prefer sunny to semi-shaded sites, although *Lemna trisulca* can also be used in shaded areas.

Its luxuriant growth means it spreads very quickly. Duckweed is not suitable, therefore, for very small ponds, and even in bigger ponds growth should be controlled by timely and regular removal.

Although it may not be very eye-catching, it does have other advantages. Duckweed is often used to slow the formation of algae in garden ponds. It is suitable for providing shade on the surface of the water, and thus offers protection to small creatures. It also removes excess nutrients from the water, and provides food for fish and water birds.

Liatris

BLAZING STAR, BUTTON SNAKEROOT OR GAY FEATHERS

40–90 cm

❋ VII–VIII

Liatris, also called blazing star, is originally a native of the eastern United States, where it is found on the prairies and among stands of trees on dry, stony ground.

This perennial forms clumps of single, linear to lanceolate leaves, which may have fine hair. Tall stems with numerous long spikes of tufted flowers spring from the clumps. Depending on the species and variety, the flowers blaze in violet, reddish-purple, purplish-pink or white between July and August. Curiously, the flower spikes bloom from top to bottom. Blazing star may grow between 16 and 36 in (40 to 90 cm) in height. The plants enjoy a sunny site and prefer damp, humus-rich, well-drained soil. Blazing star brightens up the water garden in summer with bright colors. The cheerful, colorful flower spikes are almost magically attractive to bees and butterflies. The plant is also good for providing cut flowers.

Liatris spicata is a variety that often occurs naturally in wet places, which means it is also of interest to water gardeners. This perennial plant bears its long-lasting, pinkish-purple or white flower heads, up to a half inch (1 centimeter) wide, between July and August. Blazing star can spread up to 18 in (45 centimeters) wide across. Examples of popular varieties are the brilliant carmine red "Callepsis," violet-lilac to pinkish-purple "Kobold" (40 to 50 cm) tall), or white-flowered "Floristan Weiss" 2 to 3 ft (60 to 90 cm) tall.

Ligularia

Leopard plant or Rragwort

Ligularia is a genus with around 180 species of hardy perennials native to Europe, central, and eastern Asia. They are mainly encountered beside water, in high meadows, and on damp or wet grassland. This imposing plant's special ornamental value stems from its foliage and decorative flowers.

The relatively undemanding leopard plant loves sunny to semi-shaded positions. In keeping with its natural habitat, it prefers damp, loamy, humus- and nutrient-rich soil. In prolonged dry periods it should be watered thoroughly. These striking perennials are very popular ornamental plants for water gardens. Their bright flowers create brilliant splashes of color by the water's edge. Two examples of highly decorative species are:

▬ *LIGULARIA CLIVORUM:* this species is also known by the botanical name *Ligularia dentata,* and is commonly called the big leaf ligularia. This clump-forming perennial has heart- or kidney-shaped to rounded, green leaves. It flowers between July and September, with wide, flat-topped clusters of yellow to orange-red flowers. The plant attains heights of 2 ft 6 in to 5 ft (80 to 150 centimeters). Reddish-orange flowered "Desdemona," with purple-red

80–150 cm

✳ VII–IX

to brown foliage, is very pretty, as is yellow to orange-yellow blossomed, brown-leaved "Othello."

▬ *LIGULARIA PRZEWALSKII:* This species is also known as Shavalzki's ligularia. Its yellow flowers are arranged in slender, elongated candles. It flowers between July and August. Another of the plant's characteristics is its deeply incised, palmate, and divided leaves. This *Ligularia* achieves impressive heights of 3 to 5 ft (100 to 150 centimeters).

Lithodora diffusa

Trailing lithodora or Ccommon gromwell

15–20 cm

V–VI

Lithodora diffusa, also known as trailing lithodora, or common gromwell, is found in the wild in pine forests, on shrubby land, or even on sandy soil. This pretty, evergreen, half-hardy perennial forms cushions that reach 6 to 8 in (15 to 20 centimeters) in height. The trailing branches bear small, flat, lanceolate leaves, which are elongated to ovoid and dark green in color. Trailing lithodora is especially pretty when in bloom from May to June. It is covered all over with numerous funnel-shaped flowers, which glow pure gentian blue.

Its trailing habit means that *Lithodora diffusa* is a good ground cover plant for water gardens, or can be used to fill gaps. It also looks attractive if the shoots climb over obstacles or stones. The plant enjoys full sun best, and relishes nutrient-rich, absolutely calcium-free soil.

One of the best-known and most popular varieties is the especially profuse flowering "Heavenly Blue," with its very beautiful blue flowers. "Grace Ward" has particularly large, deeply colored flowers, and the "Alba" flowers are white.

Lobelia cardinalis

Cardinal flower or Indian pink

The genus *Lobelia* comprises around 370 different species of annual, hardy, or half-hardy perennials that are distributed throughout tropical and temperate zones worldwide, especially in America. Depending on the species or variety, the plants prefer different habitats, from bogs, damp meadows, or river banks, to hilly terrain, mountain slopes, and deserts.

What follows is restricted to the species that are suitable for water gardens, where the decorative flower heads are among the most popular ornamental plants. They look superb by the edge of standing or flowing water, or in the transitional area between boggy ground and water.

Popular species

- *LOBELIA CARDINALIS:* This species, also known as the cardinal flower, naturally occurs on river and pond banks, and on boggy meadows in North America. It takes its name from the brilliant red flowers that provide bright splashes of color from June to September. The plant's leaves are narrow ovate to elongated lanceolate in

45–90 cm

VI–IX

shape, and green to brownish-red. Overall *Lobelia cardinalis* attains heights of 2 to 3 ft (60 to 90 cm). Although the plant prefers a damp and cool site, and wet to boggy soil, it loves lots of sun. It will also flourish in shallow water up to 4 in (10 centimeters).

LOBELIA FULGENS: This species is also known by the Latin name *Lobelia splendens* and the common name scarlet lobelia. Between June and September its scarlet blossoms are a highly decorative addition to a water garden. The equally attractive, lanceolate leaves are dark green, often splashed with red. *Lobelia fulgens* grows to 18 to 36 in (45 to 90 cm) in height. This plant prefers a sunny site and nutrient-rich, friable soil. One of the most popular varieties is "Queen Victoria." This member of royalty adorns itself with scarlet flowers and deep reddish-brown leaves.

Lysimachia

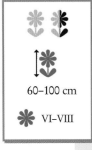

60–100 cm

VI–VIII

CREEPING CHARLIE, CREEPING JENNY OR MONEYWORT

Lysimachia is a genus with about 150 different hardy or half-hardy perennials that are native to Europe, Asia, North America, and South Africa. They mainly grow on damp grass-land, in woods, or by water. A species that is very suitable for water gardens is *Lysimachia punctata*, also known as golden globes, or garden loosestrife. It is easy to care for, and flowers profusely for a long time.

This erect, fuzzy perennial grows between 2 and 3 ft (60 to 100 cm) high. It has elliptical to lanceolate, dark green leaves and carries its dense panicles of decorative yellow flowers from June to August.

Garden loosestrife prefers a partially shaded position, where it combines well with grasses, ferns, or monk's hood. Because the plants are rhizomatous and therefore spread quickly, they should only be used in big beds, or the clumps should be divided at the right time to prevent too vigorous growth. This really undemanding, robust plant is very popular in water gardens. It is very well suited to planting along the water's edge, where its bright yellow flowers provide touches of vibrant color.

Lythrum salicaria

LOOSESTRIFE

With its splendid, reddish-purple flowers, *Lythrum salicaria*, also called loosestrife, is a wonderful sight to behold in a water garden. This plant is originally native to Europe, Asia, and southern Australia, where it is mainly found in water meadows, on banks, or in ditches. The lanceolate leaves on the upright, branching stalks are reminiscent of willow leaves. The decorative flowers, which are arranged in whorls and are grouped in long spikes, appear between July and September. The range of colors extends from purple, to pink, to carmine red.

Lythrum salicaria loves a wet to damp site and will also tolerate slight flooding to a depth of up to 6 in (15 cm). This easy-to-care-for plant prefers nutrient-rich soil and enjoys full sun or partial shade.

50–150 cm

VII–IX

Loosestrife is especially popular in water gardens because of its long flowering period and striking blooms, and is indispensable planting for any pond. In keeping with where it occurs naturally, it is superb when planted along the banks of standing or flowing water. When cut back after the main flowering period, new flowers appear again in the fall.

POPULAR SPECIESVARIETIES

- '"FEUERKERZE"': This variety has bright pink flowers and can achieve 3 to 5 ft (100 to 150 cm) in height.

- '"ROCKET"': A deep rose red variety that only reaches 2 ft 6 in (80 cm).

- '"ROBERT"': This brilliant carmine red flowered variety is also suitable for smaller gardens, because it only grows to heights of 2 to 3 ft (60 to 80 cm).

- '"ZIGEUNERBLUT"': This variety has strong, dark red flowers, and grows to around 4 ft (120 cm).

Magnolia liliiflora

300–400 cm

IV–VI

Magnolia

The genus *Magnolia* comprises more than 100 species of deciduous and evergreen trees and shrubs, which are particularly prized for their strikingly attractive, perfumed blossoms.

One example of a very decorative species is *Magnolia liliiflora*, originally native to China. This bushy, deciduous shrub bears goblet-shaped, dark red flowers. They appear between April and June. The plant's leaves are elliptical to inverted ovate, and dark green in color. Although this species of magnolia only grows very slowly, after several years it can reach a heights 9 to 13 ft of (300 to 400 centimeters).

One well-known and very commonly cultivated variety is "Nigra," whose growth is somewhat more compact than in the wild. Its leaves are dark green on top, with pale undersides. The goblet-shaped flowers appear from May to June at the same time as the leaf shoots, and are very dark reddish-purple. This plant is also suitable for small gardens because of its slow growth and compact shape.

In a water garden, this attractive plant prefers a sheltered, sunny, to partially shaded site, with damp soil that is well drained and humus rich.

Mentha aquatica

WATER OR BOG MINT

As the name suggest, *Mentha aquatica*, also known as water mint, or bog mint, is found in the wild beside water, in bogs, or in ditches. It is originally native to Europe, Asia, and Africa.

An important characteristic of water mint is its typical, aromatic, peppermint scent which, as with all species of mint, can be ascribed to the high essential oil content. This plant, which puts out runners, grows to around 8 to 24 in (20 to 60 cm) high, and bears ovoid to elliptical leaves that are dark green, sometimes splashed with reddish-brown.

DECORATIVE LEAVES

The leaves are suitable for garnishing desserts such as mousses, or fruit tarts, or can be used to flavor colorful summer salads.

The decorative flowers that appear between June and October stand in compact, spherical heads, and may be pale violet to pinkish violet.

Water mint is very versatile in water gardens, and is suitable for the boggy areas of ponds, pools, or slow-flowing water. The plant prefers a damp to wet location, in full sun to partial shade, and will even grow in shallow water up to 4 in (10 cm) deep. Because water mint tends to grow rampant, it should be kept under control by occasional thinning out.

20–60 cm

VI–X

Menyanthes trifoliata

Bog bean

15–30 cm

V–VI

In the past, *Menyanthes trifoliata* was used to treat fever, although its anti-pyrexiac properties have not been proven scientifically. In addition, the bitter compounds that the plant contains are said to have an appetite-boosting and stomach-strengthening effect. Bog bean was originally distributed throughout bogs and moors, or by ponds and rivers, in the northern hemisphere's temperate and Arctic zones.

The plant's rich green, basal broadleaves, which are divided into three leaflets, are reminiscent of clover leaves, and rise up on long stems. The fringed, white to pale pink flowers, which appear between May and June, are particularly decorative. Bog bean grows between 6 to 12 in (15 to 30 cm) in height.

Menyanthes trifoliata is happiest in a sunny to semi-shaded site, where it grows well in wet or waterlogged, practically calcium-free muddy soil, and thus will tolerate complete flooding. The depth of water should not be more than 4 to 8 in (10 to 20 cm), though, so that the plant makes a good visual impact. Bog bean fits well into the bog areas of standing or flowing water.

Mimulus

Musk

In the wild, musk, originally a native of North America, is found on banks, by springs, and in water meadows. Its decorative golden yellow flowers are especially striking. The plant grows reaches 12 to 16 in (30 to 40 cm) in height, and has lanceolate, thin, oblong or inverse lanceolate, green, serrated leaves. The flowers appear from June to August.

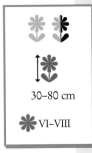

30–80 cm

✳ VI–VIII

Mimulus luteus likes damp soil best. It is also suitable for planting in shallows, although the depth of water should not exceed 2 to 4 in (5 to 10 cm). This plant prefers sunny sites, but will normally grow in partial shade too. In the water garden musk will grow well in damp areas beside the water's edge. If planted between rushes, reeds, or sedges, the bright yellow flowers are a brilliant contrast against the green of the grasses. An attractive, architectural effect can also be achieved if it is combined with flat, spreading, yellow creeping jenny or moneywort.

Other attractive species are bright red *Mimulus cardinalis* up to 16 inches (40 cm) tall and blue-violet flowering *Mimulus ringens*, which attains heights of 2 ft 6 in (80 cm).

Miscanthus sinensis

Zebra grass

Zebra grass comes into its own when most of the plants in the garden have finished flowering. The flower spikes appear in late summer or fall, and remain throughout the winter. Also, this elegant grass, with its reddish-brown foliage, is very attractive in winter.

"Silberfeder" is a very popular variety of zebra grass. It flowers profusely, with panicles that are initially reddish, then turn to silver. This clump-forming, upright plant forms large bushes, and grows to 8 ft (250 cm).

The blue-green leaves are narrow, slightly drooping, and carry a white mid-rib. This fully frost-resistant plant is not especially demanding, but prefers a sunny site and a nutrient-rich, preferably dry soil.

"Silberfeder," with its graceful, particularly large fronds of flowers, is really eye-catching. Room should be made in every water garden for this high-impact grass. As well as being planted as a single specimen, it can also be used a natural cover for the banks of garden ponds, creating beautiful reflections in the water. Highly recommended for planting with *Veronicastrum*

150 – 250 cm

VIII–X

(culver's root), *Verbena bonariensis* (purpletop verbena), *Helenium* (sneezewort), *Helianthus* (sunflower), and asters.

Molinia caerulea

Purple moorgrass

50–150 cm

✳ VIII–X

Moorgrass is very popular because of its radiantly beautiful appearance in the fall. It provides color in the water garden even this late in the year, with its decorative shades of yellow and golden brown.

This attractive, bushy grass forms compact clumps with flat, elongated linear, green leaves. The flower spikes, which appear between August and October, have purple and yellow stalks. The plant grows from around 1 ft 6 in to 5 ft (50 to 150 cm) high. Moorgrass grows well in full sun or partial shade. The soil should be damp, but well drained.

Molinia caerulea is well suited to use in water meadows where, planted in combination with meadowsweet, yarrow, or great burnet, it creates a pleasing, colorful display. The plant also does well by the water's edge, in inlets, or planted around the perimeter of stands of trees. The long flower spikes are very decorative in fresh or dried flower arrangements.

Well-known varieties are "Moorhexe," with dark spikes that reach around 1 ft 6 in (50 cm), as well as "Variegata" at 2 ft (60 cm) high, with variegated white and green leaves.

Myosotis palustris

True water forget-me-not

Myosotis palustris is mainly encountered in boggy, damp places, such as river and pond banks, in ditches, and on water meadows.

This erect perennial may grow to 1 ft (30 cm) in height, has branching stems, and has thickly haired, long, lanceolate leaves. It ornaments the water garden from May to September with its profuse heads of bright sky-blue flowers from May to September.

Water forget-me-not enjoys damp, humus-rich to loamy soils. It will also grow in shallow water up to 2 in (5 cm) in depth. It prefers a site in sun to partial shade. It looks good planted in combination with loosestrife or common arrowhead. *Myosotis palustris* is an extremely popular plant for damp areas in a garden because of its extended flowering period. Because it spreads due to creeping roots and self-seeding, it's perfect for quickly planting up blank spaces. You can create a wonderful picture by using this decorative plant along the banks of small ponds or water courses.

30 cm

V–IX

Myriophyllum

20–200 cm

VI–VIII

MILFOIL

Myriophyllum lives up to its English name, because its whorls of leaves divide into multiple, feather-like fronds. In the wild this underwater plant grows in standing or slow-flowing water.

The flower spikes, up to 6 in (15 cm) long, appear above the water's surface during the June to August flowering period. The pink to greenish-white flowers are inconspicuous. Height varies according to species, and it should be born in mind that the majority of the plant is under water.

In keeping with its natural habitat, milfoil prefers nutrient-rich, standing or slow-flowing water around 2 in (5 cm) deep. It grows best in full sun.

This underwater plant offers the garden pond many benefits. It provides protection and a habitat for many aquatic creatures, and its high level of oxygen production contributes to keeping the water clean. There follows a brief description of the three most popular species of milfoil:

■ *MYRIOPHYLLUM AQUATICUM:* This species is also known by the botanical name *Myriophyllum brasiliense*, or the common name water milfoil. It has striking blue-green leaves and originates from tropical and subtropical South America. In temperate areas it is perennial; the leaves turn red in fall. It is happy with just 2 to 4 in (5 to 10 cm) of water.

- *MYRIOPHYLLUM SPICATUM:* Also known as Eurasian water milfoil, this plant is especially popular and widespread. It is found in Europe, Asia, and Africa, as well as on Sumatra, and in the Philippines. The plant is relatively hardy and adaptable. Its leaves stand in whorls of four and, like the stems, are often flushed with red.

- *MYRIOPHYLLUM VERTICILLATUM:* This species is also known by the name whorl-leaf water milfoil. Its leaves are similar to those of the Eurasian water milfoil, but are somewhat larger and are usually arranged in five-leaved whorls. In fall, the plant forms spherical winter buds, or "pups," which sink to the pond's floor and overwinter there. In spring they then put out new shoots. The water should be at least 1 ft (30 cm) deep.

Nuphar lutea

YELLOW POND LILY, SPATTERDOCK OR BRANDY BOTTLE

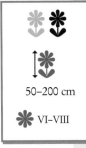

50–200 cm

VI-VIII

Nuphar lutea, also known as yellow pond lily, brandy bottle, or spatterdock, is a perennial bladder plant that is found in standing or slow-flowing water in the wild. Its beautiful yellow blooms are a wonderful addition to a large garden pond.

The plant has long-stemmed, ovate, mid- to dark-green floating leaves that have a heart-shaped curve at the heel, as well as pale green, almost translucent, underwater leaves that are wavy at the edges. Between June and August the perfumed, golden-yellow flowers rise above the water's surface on strong, 4 to 8 in (10 to 20 cm) long, strong stems. Overall the yellow pond lily grows between 1 ft 6 in and 7 ft (50 to 200 cm), with the majority of the plant being under water.

Nuphar lutea is especially happy in a sunny site, although it will grow in partial shade. Because the plant is very vigorous and needs a lot of space, the water depth should be at least 1 ft 6 in (50 to 100 cm). Thus the yellow pond lily is better suited to bigger, deeper ponds. It looks lovely when its decorative foliage is combined with other aquatic plants, such as the water lily, or yellow floating heart.

Nymphaea

Water lily

The water lily is quite simply the classic water garden plant per se, and has always entranced and inspired mankind with its elegance and grace. Because of its striking and fascinating appearance it is often described as the queen of aquatic plants. Undoubtably, it is one of the best known and most popular representatives of water flora, and should be included in every garden pond.

The decorative flowers and floating leaves are a wonderful sight and can transform any body of still water into a splendid, often pleasantly perfumed sea of flowers.

The full beauty of any water lily's flowers will be seen to best advantage in a sheltered site, in full sun, on still water. Most are suitable, therefore, for the deeper parts of a garden pond, although dwarf varieties may even be grown in shallow waters.

The various species and varieties of water lily make wonderful combinations, creating picturesque, colorful carpets of flowers on the pond's surface. Water lilies' broadleaved foliage should not cover more than one third of the water's surface, though, so that the underwater plants in the garden pond receive

20–250 cm

V–IX

enough light. There are around 50 different species of water lily distributed around the world.

Popular species

━━ *NYMPHAEA ALBA*: This white species of water lily is common throughout Europe, Asia, and North Africa. As the name suggests, it bears white, pleasantly perfumed flowers between May and September, which open in sunlight so that the golden-yellow stamens are visible. The long stemmed, rigid, floating leaves are rounded and dark green. The plants can stand in water up to 7 ft (200 cm) deep without any problem.

▪ *NYMPHAEA ODORATA*: Also called the perfumed water lily because of its pleasant scent, it bears its white, sometimes pink or yellow flowers, from May to September. It should be planted in water 1 ft 6 in to 4 ft (40 to 120 cm) deep. A very popular variety of this species is "Sulphurea" (left), with its sulfur-yellow flowers and golden-yellow stamens, it is suitable for water 2 to 3 ft (70 to 100 cm) in depth.

▬ *NYMPHAEA* "ESCARBOUCLE": This is a very decorative cultivar, whose carmine to ruby-red flowers appear from June to September, with dark orange stamens and white, pointed outer leaves. This variety is suitable for water 2 to 3 ft (50 to 100 cm) in depth.

▬ *NYMPHAEA* "JAMES BRYDON": This popular variety is also a cultivar. Between June and September it bears spherical, vivid pink to scarlet flowers with orange stamens. It will grow in waters 1 to 3 ft (40 to 80 cm deep). The shallower the water level, the wider it spreads. In good conditions water lilies soon grow subsidiary plants and can take over smaller garden ponds in just a few years. We therefore recommend sinking young plants in containers weighted with stones.

Monet's garden at Giverny

The wonderful water lily paintings by French artist Claude Monet are world famous. The Impressionist painter took his inspiration from a pond with water lilies that he had installed in his garden in Giverny (53 miles / 85 kilometers west of Paris). He returned to this theme time and again, painting around 100 versions in every conceivable light. The pond and water lilies became the subject of his paintings to the exclusion of almost any other theme. Today, Monet's garden, with its fascinating water garden, is a tourist magnet, and it offers a wealth of ideas for creating your own personal heaven on earth.

Nymphoides peltata

FLOATING HEART

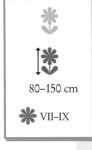

80–150 cm

❋ VII–IX

Nymphoides peltata, known as floating heart, is encountered in standing, or slow-flowing, and nutrient-rich water. This plant with floating leaves is found from Europe to eastern Asia.

Floating heart bears on its mass of stems round to heart-shaped, green, floating leaves that look like little water lily leaves on its mass of stems. Between July and September the plant is especially attractive as its ornamental, trumpet-shaped, brilliant golden-yellow flowers appear. It grows to 3 to 5 ft (80 to 150 cm) in height, with most of it growing under water, and the flowers standing about 4 in (10 cm) above the water's surface.

Nymphoides peltata loves sunny places, in still to slow-flowing water, around 8 in to 5 ft (20 to 150 cm) deep. The floor should be loamy and rich in nutrients. This decorative plant is extremely well-suited to garden ponds. Over time it can become extremely vigorous and spread widely, so in smaller ponds growth should be controlled. It looks lovely when planted with water lilies, for example.

Orontium aquaticum

Golden club

10–40 cm

IV–VI

Orontium aquaticum, colloquially known as golden club because of its golden yellow flower spike, is native to the eastern United States, where it is mostly found in bogs and stretches of water.

This perennial plant has an attractive appearance. Its elongated or narrow oval leaves are dark green, with a matte silvery sheen. If the water level is high the leaves float on the water's surface; if it is low they stand upright.

The little spears of golden yellow flowers appear from April to June, on long, thick, white stalks. The overall height is 4 to 16 in (10 to 40 cm), although part of the plant is under water.

In a water garden, this decorative plant looks particularly nice in the boggy areas of standing or slow-flowing water. It can be used effectively even in smaller ponds. It prefers full sun and a loamy, humus- and nutrient-rich soil. Golden club grows best in shallow water between 4 to 12 in (10 to 30 cm) in depth. Depending on the location, it makes a good combination planted with marsh marigold, bog bean, water forget-me-not, mare's tail, frogbit, or iris.

Penstemon barbatus

80–150 cm

VII–IX

Beardlip penstemon

The genus *Penstemon* comprises around 250 species of deciduous and evergreen, hardy, and half-hardy perennials. One extremely pretty species is *Penstemon barbatus*.

This erect perennial has lanceolate to linear, frosted, mid-green leaves. Long, slender, pyramid-shaped panicles of flowers with pendulous, tubular blooms develop between July and September. The range of colors is mostly in the spectrum of red to pink, and the plant achieves a height of 3 to 5 ft (80 to 150 cm).

Beardlip penstemons grow especially well in a sunny site. They also prefer rich, permeable soil. In areas subject to frost, the plant should be protected by covering with a thick layer of dry mulch, for example.

In a water garden, the attractive flower heads make this an extremely popular ornamental plant. They are especially well suited to brightening up the water's edge, where the fascinating, bright flowers ensure a decorative and cheerful splash of color.

Phormium

New Zealand flax

As can be deduced from the name, *Phormium* is a native of New Zealand, where it is found in brush and bogs, on slopes, and on the banks of rivers from the coast to the mountains.

Phormium is clump-forming, with elongated, tapering leaves whose colors range from yellow to dark green. There are different varieties, some of which are especially prized for their impressive, decorative foliage. The plant's little tubular flowers appear in upright panicles from August to September. New Zealand flax can reach an impressive overall height of 3 to 13 ft (100 to 400 cm).

The plant grows best in fertile, damp, permeable soil: in other words, in water gardens. It also prefers a position in full sun.

One particularly decorative variety is *Phormium* "Burgundi" (purple fountain grass), also known by the botanical name *Pennisetum setaceum* "Rubrum." This ornamental grass grows to around 3 to 4 ft (100 to 120 cm), and is especially attractive because of its burgundy-colored stems and dark red flowers.

100–400 cm

VIII-IX

Phyllitis scolopendrium

HART'S TONGUE FERN

8–40 cm

Phyllitis scolopendrium, also known as hart's tongue fern, is widely distributed throughout many parts of the northern hemisphere's temperate zones. A peculiarity of the hart's tongue fern is its solid-edged, non-pinnate leaf frond. This distinguishes it from all other European ferns, which mostly have uni- to multipinnate fronds.

Ferns are useful architectural plants for water gardens. The evergreen hart's tongue fern is especially interesting for semi-shaded to shaded spots in the garden. The new leaves produced in late spring are bright pale green, whilest the older leaves are a stronger green and are leather-like.

Phyllitis scolopendrium is best positioned on shady banks, where it looks especially good, and also finds suitable growing conditions.

It is happiest in calcium-bearing, humus-rich, and water-logged ground and, depending on the variety, may reach heights of 3 to 16 in (8 to 40 cm). Well-known varieties include "Angustifolia," with very dark green fronds that are 1 to 1 ½ in (2 to 4 cm) wide and 16 in (40 cm) long; "Capitata," with box-

like, 10 in (25 cm) long fronds; or "Crispa," with fronds that
have wavy edges.

Phyllostachys nigra

Black-jointed bamboo

300–500 cm

Phyllostachys nigra, also called black-jointed bamboo, is originally native to eastern China. This robust plant may achieve an impressive height of 10 to 16 ft (300 to 500 cm).

It forms short runners and the growth is rigidly upright. The external stems, branches, and shoots are soft and slightly overhanging.

In the first year, the stems are olive green, but in the second year they develop black points. Over the years they finally turn shiny black, which explains the plant's name. The lanceolate leaves are brilliant green on top, with a bluish underside striped green at the edge.

Phyllostachys nigra prefers fertile soil that is damp but well drained. This hardy plant grows best in a sunny to partially shaded position.

With its elegant shape and decorative foliage, black-jointed bamboo is a popular ornamental plant for water gardens. It is suitable for use as a single specimen, or in borders, and can be put to good use as a screening plant. When combined with yellow- or green-stemmed bamboo, it is possible to create dense and interesting architectural patterns, especially as a background to a pond.

Physostegia

False dragonhead or Oobedient plant

Physostegia gets the common name of obedient plant from the fact that its single blooms sit on little hinges and when moved, remain where placed. The plant is originally native to North America.

One of the best known species, which can also be used to good effect in a water garden, is *Physostegia virginiana*. This hardy perennial reaches 2 to 3 ft (60 to 100 cm) in height, and bears elliptical, lanceolate, or spade-shaped, mid-green leaves, with sharply toothed edges. During the flowering period of July to September, the dense candles of pink, dark purple, or white flowers appear. Popular varieties include white-flowering "Alba" and "Summer Snow," pinkish-purple flowering "Variegata," or reddish-pink to purplish-pink "Vivid."

The obedient plant prefers a sunny to semi-shaded position, with fertile, damp, and well-drained soil. It is sensitive to long periods of drought, and should be given additional waterings as necessary. In water gardens this plant is superb for the water's edge, where its unusual and attractive flower spikes are sure to catch the eye.

60–100 cm

VII–IX

Pistia stratiotes

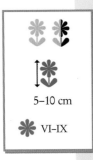

5–10 cm

✹ VI–IX

Water lettuce

Because it is reminiscent of a head of lettuce in shape, *Pistia stratiotes* is also called water lettuce. This floating plant is originally native to tropical and subtropical regions around the world.

The most striking characteristic of the perennial water lettuce is its attenuated, bluish to pale green leaves, which stand in a very compact rosette that lies on the water. The surface appears soft and velvety because of fine, water-repellant hairs. On the other hand, the little, white to greenish flowers, which emerge at the leaf joints between June and September, are inconspicuous and are mostly overlooked. The plant generally reaches a height of 2 to 4 in (5 to 10 cm).

Pistia stratiotes grows best in shallow, sunny to partially shaded waters, at a depth of 6 to 10 in (15 to 25 cm). The plant grows more luxuriantly if the roots can reach the floor than if they float free in the water. In extremely warm summer weather it can spread so quickly with its runners that it might be necessary to thin it out. Because it is only half-hardy, as it is a tropical plant, water lettuce should be overwintered in a warm, bright location, as necessary.

In water gardens, this attractive floating plant does especially well in the boggy and marginal areas of still garden ponds. It can be planted in combination with water hyacinth, water soldier, or water lily.

Polemonium reptans

JACOB'S LADDER

Polemonium, also called Jacob's ladder, or Greek valerian, is a genus with various species of perennials and annuals, which occur in Europe, Asia, North and Central America. It is found in stony or alpine areas, as well as beside water courses, or in water meadows, stands of woodtrees, or on shrub land. These beautiful plants are especially popular because of their pinnate leaves and attractive bell-, cup-, or trumpet-shaped flowers.

One very pretty species, which originates in North America, is *Polemonium reptans*, which is also known as creeping Jacob's ladder. The plant grows to 12 to 16 in (30 to 40 cm), and bears its pendulous blue flowers, in loose, flat-topped heads, from May to July. This decorative plant is well- suited to adding interest to banks and the edges of damp woodland, or areas of perennials in water gardens. Jacob's ladder prefers a site in full sun or partial shade. It grows best in moist to damp, well-drained, humus-rich soil.

One of the best known varieties is "Blue Pearl," with its especially striking, azure flowers (right).

30–40 cm

V–VII

Polygonum

Smartweed

There are many species of *Polygonum*, including annuals, perennials, and a few half-hardy perennials. They may be evergreen, or deciduous, and occur in a wide range of habitats.

Popular species

- *POLYGONUM AMPHIBIUM:* This species is also called water smartweed, because it can grow both on land, and in deep water, or boggy areas. The land version of the plant may grow to 1 to 2 ft (30 to 50 cm) in height. The aquatic form, which grows 1 to 10 ft (30 to 300 cm) under the water, is a highly decorative addition to water gardens. The shiny, long-stemmed floating leaves are extremely ornamental. The spikes of numerous pink flowers appear between June and September and may conjure a veritable sea of flowers on the surface of standing or slow-flowing water. Water smartweed grows best in full sun, or in a partially shaded site close to water.

- *POLYGONUM AMPLEXICAULE* (left and right): This species, also known as mountain fleece, grows between 3 to 4 ft (100 to 120 cm). It originated in the Himalayas. Between July and October the long-stemmed, slender spikes develop bright red flowers. In the fall, the plant makes a valuable contribution of color to semi-semishaded and damp locations.

- *POLYGONUM BISTORTA:* Mainly distributed in Europe and Asia, it is also called meadow bistort. It is well suited to damp banks beside water, or beds with heavy soiled beds, and reaches 1 to 3 ft (40 to 100 cm) in height. The long, reddish to white flower spikes appear between May and September.

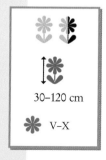

30–120 cm

V–X

Polystichum setiferum

Holly fern

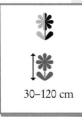

30–120 cm

Ferns are some of the oldest plants known to man. Countless versions are found growing wild all over the world. They are indispensable in water gardens for adding greenery to lightly and deeply shaded places.

Polystichum setiferum is also called holly fern, and is one of the most elegant species. It forms funnel-shaped, spreading bushes and its stalks are covered in scales and hairs. This ever-green plant is especially attractive because of its filigree fronds. They are multi-pinnate, matte green, and soft. This bushy plant attains heights of 1 to 3 ft (30 to 80 cm), but in the right growing conditions, and with solicitous care, may even grow to 4 ft (120 cm). *Plumosum densum* is a very attractive variety.

Holly fern prefers partial shade, but if there is enough mois-ture, it will also grow in places away from the sun. It enjoys moist, humus- and nutrient-rich soil, and the effect when plant-ed at the water's edge is very pleasing.

Pontederia cordata

60–100 cm

VI–IX

Pickerel weed

Pontederia cordata, also known by the name pickerel weed, is originally a native of the eastern United States, where it is found in bogs and areas of shallow water. Its eye-catching racemes of many tiny, pale blue, individual flowers, there to be admired between June and September, make pickerel weed one of the most popular ornamental plants. No less attractive are its long-stemmed, heart-shaped to lanceolate green leaves. *Pontederia cordata* may grow to 2 to 3 ft (60 to 100 cm).

This warmth-loving plant prefers wet, muddy soil that is as free of calcium as possible. It especially enjoys a very sunny position, but will also tolerate partial shade. It grows best in 6 to 12 in (15 to 30 cm) of water. Additional protection is recommended in very cold winters, or overwintering away from possible frosts.

Pickerel weed flowers very profusely, and can be a truly spectacular sight in a water garden. It is well suited to boggy areas or shallows at the margins of ponds, or slow-flowing streams. Achieve a colorful effect by planting alongside flowering rush, purple loosestrife, or frogbit.

Primula

PRIMROSES OR PRIMULAS

Together with snowdrops and crocuses, primroses are among the most well-beloved heralds of spring. After the dismal grey of winter, they provide cheerful splashes of color in water gardens.

The genus *Primula*, from the Latin for "first," is immense, comprising around 550 species. Without exception they are delicate and graceful plants, which usually take the form of rosette-shaped perennial clumps, from which the flower stalks rise. These bear individual, or even profusely flowering heads of individual flowers, which are tubular to plate shaped.

The primroses described below are two examples of decorative species that are well suited to water gardens, where they adorn the banks of standing or flowing water, for example, with their bright, cheerful colors. Both species introduced here grow best in moist, humus-syrich soil, and in partially shaded positions where, if there is enough moisture, they will also tolerate a little more sun.

POPULAR SPECIES

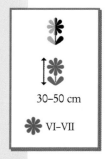

30–50 cm

VI–VII

- *PRIMULA JAPONICA (LEFT):* This species is called English primrose. Its whorls of flowers are arranged in tiers and sit on long stems. They appear from June to July. Different colors of this perennial plant are available, with the color spectrum going from purple, to red, to pink shades, to white. These primulas grow to around 20 in (50 cm). Recommended varieties for water gardens are carmine red "Atropurpurea" and brilliant pale red "Fiery Red."

- *PRIMULA VIALII:* This is a very attractive species with wide, lance-shaped leaves rounded at the top. They are covered in hairs on both sides and irregularly toothed at the edges. The pointed cones of flower spikes appear between June and July. The unopened flowers are scarlet to carmine; when open they glow a strong lavender blue. This species grows 1 to 2 ft (30 to 50 cm).

Prunus

Ornamental cherry

Because in the wild it is native to the mountain woodlands of Japan, Korea, and Sakhalin, *Prunus sargentii* is also known as the mountain cherry. Like all ornamental cherries it is mainly cultivated for its spectacular blossom.

The spreading, deciduous tree may reach an impressive height in excess of 30 ft (10 meters). The crown is conical to widely spreading; the side branches are initially angled acutely upwards, then pendulous. The smooth bark is chestnut brown, the dark green leaves are elliptical to ovate, and they end in a long point. In autumn, the leaves turn a beautiful, bright orange or red. Between April and May the countless, cup-shaped, pale pink to reddish-pink blossoms open. Later in the year they form egg-shaped, cherry-like, shiny fruit that is red to purplish-black in color.

The beautiful blossom and dazzling fall colors make *Prunus sargentii* one of the most popular ornamental trees for water gardens. It prefers a place in full sun and will grow well in damp but well-drained, humus-rich soil.

3–10 m

IV–V

One very attractive variety is the pale pink to reddish-pink flowering "Accolade." At just 10 to 13 ft (300 to 400 cm) high, it remains relatively small and is thus ideally suited to smaller water gardens.

Pseudosasa japonica

Bamboo

Pseudosasa japonica is commonly known as bamboo. In Japan its straight stems were once used for arrows. The plant is originally native to the warm, humid areas of Japan and Korea.

Bamboo grows upright and forms thickish clumps. The plant's stems droop slightly at the top. Initially they are dark green to olive green in color, then they turn pale beige. This species of bamboo's large, wide, and relatively dense leaves are striking and, because of their dark green color, they are an attractive feature.

The leaves are silvery-grey to blue-green on the underside. In favorable conditions bamboo can reach heights of 7 to 20 ft (200 to 600 cm). This easy-to-care-for and relatively robust plant prefers fertile, damp, but well-drained soil, and a protected site in sun or partial shade. The impressive *Pseudosasa japonica* can be used to great architectural effect in water gardens. The shiny, elegantly curved leaves create an exotic atmosphere. Like many other species of bamboo, it is also ideal for acting as a screen.

200–600 cm

Rhododendron

Rhododendron

It's impossible to conceive of our parks and gardens without the splendor of a rhododendron in bloom. Many people automatically associate rhododendrons with England, because it forms bushes as high as the houses there. This plant flourishes in the United Kingdom because of the mild, foggy, oceanic climate. The rhododendron's real home though, is Asia: Japan, Sumatra, Malaysia, and especially the Himalayas, where it covers whole hillsides with luxuriant woods.

Seeds from these wild species reached Europe almost 300 years ago, and the rhododendron has continued its triumphal march ever since. Breeders experimented with it until they had made it hardy enough to withstand winters in northern Europe so, as an evergreen, it is attractive even during the cold season.

Popular species

■ *RHODODENDRON PRAECOX:* This one launches the rhododendron flowering season. In mild weather it sometimes flowers as early as February, otherwise between March and April, with bright purplish-pink flowers. The

30–200 cm

❋ II–VI

evergreen shrub has oval-shaped leaves, which are a shiny dark green with a spicy scent. Growth is loose and upright, and reaches 4 to 5 ft (120 to 150 cm). A sheltered site is important, but the shrub itself is fully winter hardy, although its blossoms are at risk from late frosts. After a frosty night, the flowers are either frozen or badly damaged. If there is a risk of late frosts, the plants should be protected with plastic wrap or fleece.

■ *RHODODENDRON HIRSUTUM:* This very twiggy, rounded shrub, which only grows to 1 to 3 ft (30 to 100 cm), has densely leaved, evergreen branches. The leaves, which are shiny bright green on top, with glandular scales underneath, are thickly fringed at the edges. In May and June the profuse, funnel- to bell-shaped flowers unfold. They are purplish-pink, with white hairs on the inside, clustered in umbels of three to ten flowers.

■ *RHODODENDRON OBTUSUM JAPONICUM:* These are Japanese azalea hybrids. As the name suggest they originate from Japan. These are deciduous shrubs that do not grow as big as the evergreen species of rhododendron. They are mostly low growing, broad, and compact and rarely exceed 3 ft (100 cm). The many different varieties bear abundant blossoms in red, orange, pink, or white. These hybrids are especially suitable for small group plantings in front of other, bigger rhododendrons.

Rhus typhina

Staghorn sumach

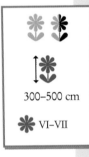

300–500 cm

VI–VII

Rhus typhina is a native of eastern North America, where it is found on different soils, but mostly in bright sites.

This large, erect, deciduous shrub can grow 10 to 17 ft (300 or to 500 cm), sometimes taller. The scantily branched boughs, covered with velvety hairs, have long and lance-shaped, pinnate leaves, which are rich green on top and pale grey-green underneath. In the fall they display a range of decorative colors, from yellow, to brilliant orange, to scarlet. The erect panicles of yellowish-green flowers open between June and July, and later ripen into club-like, thickly haired, scarlet to dark red fruits.

This decorative plant is especially good for creating colorful, picturesque scenes in the water garden in the fall. It prefers well-drained, dry to moist soil, and grows best in full sun to partial shade. A smaller, slower-growing variety that is especially suitable for water gardens is "Dissecta," which only grows between 6 and 13 ft (200 and to 400 cm) and has beautiful, finely cut leaves.

Because the staghorn sumach puts out runners very quickly, it should be sited on its own, or suitable measures should be taken to contain it, i.e. by planting inside a ring. *Rhus typhina* "Dissecta" is also suitable for use as a container plant.

Rodgersia

RODGERSFLOWER

70–100 cm

VI–VII

Rodgersia, known simply as rodgersflower, is a genus with six species of vigorous perennials that form clumps, and which are distributed throughout the temperate zones of eastern Asia. It is usually found in damp woods and beside river banks.

One very decorative species is *Rodgersia aesculifolia*, which is also known as fingerleaf rodgersflower because of its foliage. The plant bears fingered, wrinkled, bright green leaves, with five to seven serrated fronds. The stems, stalks, and leaf veins are covered with woolly, reddish-brown hairs. From June to July it develops panicles of white or pink flowers up to 2 ft (60 cm) in length. Rodgersflower attains heights of 2 to 3 ft (70 to 100 cm).

This imposing perennial is popular in water gardens for its striking, decorative foliage and large, branching panicles of flowers.

It can be placed to good effect by the water's edge, in bog gardens, or damp beds. It grows best in a partially shaded to shaded position, but if there is sufficient moisture it will also tolerate a site in full sun. The soil should be fertile, damp, and humus-rich. It can be planted with astilbes, ferns, grasses, groundsel, rhododendrons, or bugbane.

Sagittaria sagittifolia

Arrowhead

Sagittaria sagittifolia, also known as arrowhead because of the shape of its leaves, is distributed from Europe to Asia. This decorative bog perennial grows on banks, in ditches, in ponds, and in pools in the wild.

Being a relatively adaptable plant, arrowhead will cope with different depths of water. It has three types of leaves: the ribbon-shaped floating underwater leaves, the spade-shaped floating leaves, and the typical, long-stemmed, arrow-shaped leaves that rise up out of the water. The white flowers, which appear between June and July, stand on an upright flower stalk, and have a purple fleck at the base of each petal. Arrowhead grows to 2 ft (50 cm) in height.

Sagittaria sagittifolia prefers nutrient-rich waters with humus-rich, sandy, or muddy soil. The plant will tolerate water between 2 to 16 in (5 to 40 cm) deep. It loves full sun, but will grow in partial shade too. In the water garden, arrowhead is one of the most popular plants for bog areas. Plants that complement it include water plantain, flowering rush, or water mint.

40–50 cm

VI–VIII

Saponaria

Bouncingbet

This plant's botanical name reflects the fact that the saponines it contains foam like soap when placed in water. The botanical name is derived from the Latin word for soap, *sapo*. In the past bouncingbet was used as a detergent. It is also supposed to have medicinal properties, loosening mucus in the bronchial tubes, and thus helping with respiratory problems. It is also believed to be efficacious against skin rashes and eczema.

This plant, originally native to mountain slopes in southern and southeastern Europe, is mainly suitable for larger gardens, because of its spreading habit. With its mostly low-lying, decoratively leaved shoots, it usually forms spreading carpets that grow to 4 to 8 in (10 to 20 cm) high. The leaves are needle-shaped. Bouncingbet is especially attractive during the summer months of June and July, when the evergreen carpet is covered with a profusion of beautiful little flowers. These are arranged in dense cymes. The colors vary from red to pink, but there are also white-flowering varieties.

Saponaria ocymoides is a popular, rather undemanding plant. In the water garden it prefers a sunny site and grows best in moist, well-drained, calcium-rich soil. The decorative carpet of flowers is a colorful addition to the water's edge.

Well-known varieties include white-flowering "Alba," dark red, compact "Rubra compacta," or deep reddish-pink "Splendens."

10–20 cm

VI–VII

Scirpus tabernaemontani

Bulrush or club grass

Scirpus tabernaemontani also goes by the botanical name *schoeno-plectus tabernaemontani*. In the wild this plant is found in bogs, on the shores of lakes, and beside slow-flowing water.

The bulrush has stiff, grey-green stems and bears its red-dish-brown flowers between June and August. The plant grows to 4 ft (120 cm) in height. A very well-known and popular vari-ety is "Zebrinus," also called zebra rush. The name is indicative of this variety's particular characteristic: the white and green, diagonally striped stem. Bulrush is especially happy in a sunny to partially shaded site. It grows best in loamy, boggy soil and will tolerate water between 2 and 12 in (5 to 30 cm) deep. We recommend planting it in containers for smaller ponds, to inhibit rapid spread, and to keep the plant low-growing.

This decorative plant has many uses in water gardens. It is highly suitable for landscaping wildlife ponds, bog gardens, or water courses. The stems of zebra rush are especially eye-catch-ing.

60–120 cm

VI–VIII

Sparganium erectum

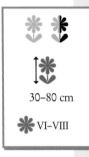

30–80 cm

VI–VIII

Simplestem bur-reed

Sparganium erectum's interesting, very decorative fruits are covered in spikes, or burs. This attractive bog plant originates from bodies of standing water in Europe and Asia.

Sparganium erectum has branching flower stalks and bears yellowish green, grassy, sword-shaped broadleaves. The plant is extremely vigorous and grows 1 to 3 ft (30 to 80 cm). From June to August little white, rather ordinary flowers appear at the junctions of the primary bracts.

The undemanding simple stem bur-reed prefers sunny or shaded sites. It grows well at the water's edge with a muddy, nutrient-rich floor, and will tolerate water up to 1 ft (30 cm deep). Because this plant tends to spread rapidly via runners, it is more suitable for larger ponds. In smaller areas of water it should be planted in containers that restrict spread. In the water garden *Sparganium erectum* is good for the shallow, marginal areas of garden ponds. It looks very nice combined successfully with cattails, or pickerel weed.

Stachys grandiflora

Big betony

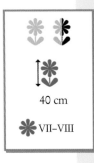

40 cm

✺ VII–VIII

The genus *Stachys* comprises around 300 species of annual, hardy or half-hardy perennial plants that are widespread, especially in the northern temperate zones.

A highly decorative species is *Stachys grandiflora*, also called big betony, which is native to the Caucasus Mountains, in northeastern Turkey, and northwestern Iran. The erect, hairy perennial forms rosettes of widely ovate, indented, wrinkled, long-stemmed, dark green leaves. Compact whorls of big purplish-pink false spikes of flowers appear on erect stalks between July and August. The plant grows to 16 in (40 cm).

In water gardens this hardy perennial's striking flowers are really striking, providing brilliant splashes of color. This plant grows best in a site in full sun, but will tolerate partial shade. The soil should be free-draining and moderately fertile. If the conditions are right, this plant will quickly form clumps. Examples of well-known varieties are "Superba," with darker purple-pink to lilac-pink flowers, or pink-flowering "Rosea."

Stipa barbata

Feathergrass

Stipa barbata, also called feathergrass, originated in temperate to tropical dry zones.

This plant is particularly ornamental because of its wheat-like panicles of flowers, with pendulous, curved, feathery beards up to 1 ft (40 cm) in length. They shimmer like silver silk, and move like feathers in the slightest breath of wind. The narrow, grey-green leaves are also extremely effective, forming clumps up to 2 ft 6 in (80 cm) high.

This plant prefers a warm, sunny location on dry, chalky, free-draining soil. It is relatively easy to care for, but is sensitive to wet in winter. The graceful flower stalks that sway gently in the breeze are perfect for creating architectural plantings in water gardens. The effect is especially lovely when feathergrass is planted in groups. When combined with blue-flowering sage or veronica it is also displayed to good advantage, and the fruit heads are also very attractive for use in bouquets.

80 cm

VI–VIII

Stratiotes aloides

WATER SOLDIER

Stratiotes aloides is also commonly known as crab's claw, because the flowers' two spatheous bracts look like the claws of a crab or lobster. Because its fleshy, sword-shaped and jagged-edged leaves are reminiscent of the aloe, the plant is also known by the name water aloe. It is widespread in standing and slow-flowing water from Europe to northern Asia.

A particular feature of water soldier is that, in the fall, it sinks down to the pond's floor, where the axillary shoots lie for the whole winter. Only in spring do they rise again to just beneath the water's surface, and finally rise out of the water during the flowering season of May to September, when the three-petalled white flowers appear on the thick stalks.

In deeper water *Stratiotes aloides* is free floating. In shallower water the long roots are anchored in the ground. It propagates by rhizomes, or pups, and may become so prolific that it has to be thinned out, to prevent it spreading too much. Although the plant only reaches 6 to 16 in (15 to 40 cm) in height, it is mostly submerged, and only stands about 1 ft (30 cm) above the water during the flowering season.

In the water garden the decorative water soldier is superb for calm ponds, where it paints a scenic picture with its leaves rising above the water's surface. It can also be planted in very slow-flowing water, but it should stand in a shallow, calm place where it can anchor its roots. This winter-hardy plant does extremely well in low-calcium, nutrient-rich water. It loves a sunny site, preferably sheltered from the wind, but may grow in partial shade, depending on the conditions.

15–40 cm

V–IX

Taxodium distichum

Bald-cypress

Taxodium distichum, also called bald-cypress, is a slender, tall tree which loses its needles in winter. It is originally a native of south-eastern North America, mainly Texas and Florida.

The tree's roots spread out like a board and it has pale brown, fibrous bark. The needles are lance-shaped and pale green; in the fall they turn rusty red, before they fall off with the short shoots. *Taxodium distichum* achieves an impressive height of 60 to 120 ft (20 to 40 meters). A particular feature of the tree is its roots, or knees. These are roots up to 5 ft (150 cm) high, which rise up out of the root space, water, or soil and provide the tree with sufficient oxygen.

Bald-cypress grows well in damp to moist soil, and prefers full sun or partial shade. It will also grow in shallow water. Like most conifers, because of its size bald-cypress is really only suitable for bigger gardens or parks. It is very decorative as a single specimen for architectural use in a water garden.

20–40 m

Thalictrum aquilegifolium

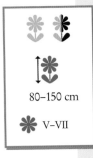

80–150 cm

V–VII

Meadow rue

The different species of rue are native to the northern hemisphere, tropical South America, and southern Africa. A good species for water gardens is *Thalictrum aquilegifolium*, also called meadow rue.

Meadow rue reaches heights of 3 to 5 ft (80 to 150 cm) and bears bi- or tri-pinnate, shiny, blue-green leaves. The flowers, which rise above the foliage on tall elegant stems, are impressive. They look like beautiful bushes of feathers because of their countless stamens arranged in a ball. They appear between May and July, and may be pink to pale lilac, white, or violet.

This undemanding plant prefers a sunny or partially shaded place. The soil should be moist to damp, and humus-rich. In a water garden *Thalictrum aquilegifolium* is best placed by the damp edge of the pool, but it is also suitable for boggy areas. It looks striking and extremely decorative planted in groups with grasses, golden globes, or iris.

Trapa natans

Water chestnut

5–20 cm

VI-IX

Trapa natans, or water chestnut, originally occurs in standing water from Europe, Asia, to North Africa. In Germany the plant is threatened with extinction and is a protected species. The water chestnut's fruit is edible and was known as a foodstuff in the Stone Age.

This annual water plant is attractive because of its floating rosettes of diamond-shaped, dark green leaves. Over the summer the leaves turn brilliant red and so provide splashes of color until the fall. The little white flowers that appear between June and September are, on the other hand, rather inconspicuous. They turn into half-inch (2 cm) square, thorny, black fruits. When the plant dies back in the fall, the fruits sink to the pond floor. In the following spring they may form new plants, but only in very favorable growing conditions, combined with optimum soil and water temperatures. The water chestnut needs a site in warm, standing water, which should preferably be 8 to 20 in (20 to 50 cm) deep. It grows best in full sun, but can tolerate partially shaded sites.

Trollius

Globe flower

Trollius, also known as globe flower, is originally native to the cool, temperate latitudes of Europe, Asia, and North America, where it is found in damp and wet grassland.

The spherical, sometime bowl-shaped flower head is characteristic of this attractive plant. Depending on the species and variety, the colors range from pale yellow to deep orange. The leaves are palmate, divided, and a medium green.

Globe flower likes a sunny or partially shaded position best, and prefers humus-rich or loamy soil. In extended dry periods, care should be taken to water it regularly so the rootstock does not dry out.

In the water garden this decorative plant is ideally suited to brightening up the banks of ponds or streams. It can also provide splashes of bright color in damp meadows. Combine with iris, marsh marigold, or grasses, to create very attractive planting.

▬ *TROLLIUS CHINENSIS* (left): Blooming from June to July, Chinese globe flower continues flowering where the European globe flower leaves off. It grows to 3 ft (90 cm). The orange flowers are open and bowl- to cup-shaped, which is how it can be distinguished from the European globe flower. One well-known variety is "Golden Queen," whose bright orange flowers are very striking.

▬ *TROLLIUS EUROPAEUS:* This native European globe flower may reach 4 in to 3 ft (10 to 90 cm) in height. It bears yellow, spherical flowers from May to June. "Superbus," attaining around 2 ft (50 to 60 cm) in height, is a popular variety with pale yellow flowers.

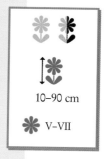

10–90 cm

V–VII

Typha

CATTAIL

Typha, also known as the cattail, is often found in the wild in nutrient-rich ponds or lakes, in pools or ditches, and in slow-flowing water.

Cattail species are perennial plants with rather inconspicuous flowers that appear from June to August. The plants are very popular because of their decorative, mostly deep brown clubs that form in late summer.

Typha prefers a very sunny, warm site, but will cope with partial shade too. This plant grows best in the reed beds of standing water that is around 8 to 16 in (20 to 40 cm) deep. *Typha minima*, or dwarf cattail, should not, however, stand in water more than 2 to 4 in (5 to 10 cm) deep.

Because cattails spread quickly and can completely take over a pond, we recommend planting them in containers, to limit spread. In addition to its decorative value, the undemanding and easy-to-care-for cattails have other benefits for garden ponds. They help to clarify water by removing nutrients and are important for oxygen management.

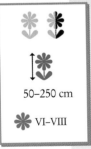

50–250 cm

VI-VIII

YPHA ANGUSTIFOLIA: This has narrow leaves and bears long, slender clubs, which tower over the leaves and achieve a considerable height of 5 to 7 ft (150 to 200 cm).

TYPHA LATIFOLIA: This species has somewhat broader leaves. The clubs are squat, usually very dark, and tower above the foliage, reaching as high as 7 ft (200 cm).

TYPHA LAXMANNII: This species grows to about 5 ft (150 cm). The clubs are ovate and stand amongst the foliage.

TYPHA MINIMA: Also known as dwarf cattail, this is also suitable for smaller ponds and ditches because of its smaller height of just 20 to 30 in (50 to 80 cm). It bears almost globular clubs above its narrow leaves.

TYPHA SHUTTLEWORTHII: A particular characteristic of this species is its silver -grey clubs. It is one of the taller species, reaching heights of 3 to 7 ft (100 to 200 cm).

Viburnum sargentii

SARGENT'S VIBURNUM

The foliage, flowers, and fruit of Sargent's viburnum are highly decorative, and this is what makes the many species of the genus *Viburnum* especially popular, and frequently cultivated garden shrubs. This shrub is often called "Snowball" because of the mostly white flowers, which in many of the species stand in spherical panicles or groups.

One decorative species is *Viburnum sargentii*, native to northeast Asia. This bushy, deciduous shrub's leaves are bronze when they shoot, later turning yellow to red. The flower heads (cymes) appear between May and June, and are composed of numerous little white individual flowers. These later ripen into spherical red fruits. Overall shrub height is 7 to 10 ft (200 to 300 cm).

This hardy perennial shrub prefers a sunny or partially shaded position, and grows best in moist to damp, well-drained soil. With its decorative leaves, white flowers, and bright red fruit, *Viburnum sargentii* adorns the water garden throughout the year. It is suitable for planting beside water or on the edge of a shrubbery.

200–400 cm

✸ V–VI

A well-known variety is *Viburnum opulus*, which grows to 13 ft (400 cm), and likes a sunny or partially shaded spot in which to grow. It is usually found beside river banks and on the edge of damp woods. It also needs good air circulation to flourish.

Index of common plant names

Index of Latin plant names

Photographic acknowledgements

Jürgen Schossig: 21, 63, 77, 89; Metten Stein & Design: 23, 40, 42, 78, 81; Cane-line A/S: 26; Oase: 46, 47, 64, 83, 88, 91, 104, 10 - 110; Gardena: 49, 50, 100; Ubbink 48; OASE GmbH: 102, 103, 104, 106, 107, 108, 109, 110, 111

All other photos: Medien Kommunikation, Unna

Photographers: Hermann Hackstein, Michael Hase, Raphael Pehle

Design and production: Tobias Pehle

Assistants: Yara Hackstein, Carola Struck, Mathias Hinkerode, Dietrich Löbbecke, Raphael Pehle

Special thanks go to Martin Struck and Francis Pehle